50 Classic French Pastries Recipes for Home

By: Kelly Johnson

Table of Contents

- Croissants
- Pain au Chocolat
- Éclairs
- Tarte Tatin
- Macarons
- Palmiers
- Madeleines
- Financiers
- Chausson aux Pommes (Apple Turnovers)
- Pâte à Choux
- Profiteroles
- Galette des Rois
- Pithiviers
- Mille-Feuille
- Opera Cake
- Brioche
- Tarte aux Fruits (Fruit Tart)
- Kouign-Amann
- Paris-Brest
- Religieuse
- Gougères
- Quiche Lorraine
- Crêpes
- Cannele de Bordeaux
- Baba au Rhum
- Clafoutis
- Tarte au Citron (Lemon Tart)
- Pain Perdu (French Toast)
- Tarte Normande
- Saint-Honoré Cake
- Pissaladière
- Flan Parisien
- Tarte à l'Oignon (Onion Tart)
- Far Breton
- Pain d'Épices (French Spice Bread)

- Mousse au Chocolat
- Tartelette aux Framboises (Raspberry Tartlet)
- Gâteau Basque
- Puits d'Amour
- Choux à la Crème
- Sacristains
- Bouillabaisse Marseillaise (Fisherman's Stew)
- Tarte aux Noix (Walnut Tart)
- Navettes de Marseille
- Tarte Provençale
- Pain Complet (Whole Wheat Bread)
- Pain Poilâne
- Pain de Campagne
- Bugnes
- Pain de Mie (White Sandwich Bread)

Croissants

Ingredients:

For the Dough:

    2 1/4 teaspoons (1 packet) active dry yeast
    1/4 cup warm water (about 110°F or 43°C)
    1 cup cold milk
    1/4 cup granulated sugar
    3 cups all-purpose flour, plus more for rolling
    1 teaspoon salt
    1 cup unsalted butter, cold but pliable

For the Egg Wash:

8. 1 large egg

    1 tablespoon milk

Instructions:

1. Activate the Yeast:

- In a small bowl, dissolve the yeast in warm water and let it sit for 5-10 minutes until it becomes frothy.

2. Prepare the Dough:

- In a large mixing bowl, combine cold milk, sugar, and the activated yeast mixture. Stir well.
- Add flour and salt, mixing until a shaggy dough forms.
- Turn the dough onto a lightly floured surface and knead for a few minutes until it comes together.
- Shape the dough into a rectangle, wrap it in plastic wrap, and refrigerate for 1 hour.

3. Incorporate the Butter:

- Roll out the chilled dough into a larger rectangle.

- Flatten the cold butter between two sheets of parchment paper into a rectangle of similar size.
- Place the butter layer onto one half of the dough, then fold the other half over it.
- Seal the edges and roll out the dough again into a rectangle.

4. Create Layers:

- Perform a series of three "fold and turns" by folding the dough into thirds like a letter, chilling in between each turn for 30 minutes.

5. Shape the Croissants:

- Roll out the dough into a large rectangle and cut it into smaller rectangles or triangles.
- Roll each piece tightly from the wider end to form a classic croissant shape.
- Place the croissants on a baking sheet lined with parchment paper.

6. Rise and Preheat:

- Let the shaped croissants rise at room temperature for 2-3 hours or until doubled in size.
- Preheat your oven to 400°F (200°C).

7. Egg Wash:

- Whisk together the egg and milk to create an egg wash.
- Brush the tops of the croissants with the egg wash.

8. Bake:

- Bake in the preheated oven for 15-20 minutes or until golden brown and puffed up.
- Allow them to cool on a wire rack before serving.

Enjoy your homemade French croissants! Serve them fresh with butter, jam, or your favorite spread.

Pain au Chocolat

Ingredients:

For the Dough:

    2 1/4 teaspoons (1 packet) active dry yeast
    1/4 cup warm water (about 110°F or 43°C)
    1 cup cold milk
    1/4 cup granulated sugar
    3 cups all-purpose flour
    1 teaspoon salt
    1 cup unsalted butter, cold but pliable

For the Chocolate Filling:

8. 6 ounces (170g) good-quality dark chocolate, chopped

    2 tablespoons unsalted butter

For the Egg Wash:

10. 1 large egg

    1 tablespoon milk

Instructions:

1. Activate the Yeast:

- In a small bowl, dissolve the yeast in warm water and let it sit for 5-10 minutes until it becomes frothy.

2. Prepare the Dough:

- In a large mixing bowl, combine cold milk, sugar, and the activated yeast mixture. Stir well.
- Add flour and salt, mixing until a soft dough forms.
- Turn the dough onto a floured surface and knead for a few minutes until it's smooth.
- Wrap the dough in plastic wrap and refrigerate for 1 hour.

3. Incorporate the Butter:

- Roll out the chilled dough into a rectangle.
- Flatten the cold butter between two sheets of parchment paper into a rectangle of similar size.
- Place the butter layer onto one half of the dough, then fold the other half over it.
- Seal the edges and roll out the dough again into a rectangle.

4. Create Layers:

- Perform a series of three "fold and turns" by folding the dough into thirds like a letter, chilling in between each turn for 30 minutes.

5. Prepare Chocolate Filling:

- Melt the dark chocolate and butter together, either n a double boiler or using short bursts in the microwave.
- Allow the chocolate mixture to ccol slightly.

6. Shape Pain au Chocolat:

- Roll out the laminated dough into a large rectangle.
- Spread the chocolate mixture evenly over the dough.
- Roll the dough tightly from one of the longer edges
- Cut into 1-inch slices.

7. Rise and Preheat:

- Place the pain au chocolat on a baking sheet lined with parchment paper.
- Allow them to rise at room temperature for 1-2 hours.

- Preheat your oven to 400°F (200°C).

8. Egg Wash and Bake:

    - Whisk together the egg and milk to create an egg wash.
    - Brush the tops of the pain au chocolat with the egg wash.
    - Bake for 15-20 minutes or until golden brown.

9. Serve:

    - Allow the pain au chocolat to cool slightly before serving.

Enjoy your homemade Pain au Chocolat with a cup of coffee or tea!

Éclairs

Ingredients:

For the Choux Pastry:

   1 cup water
   1/2 cup unsalted butter
   1 cup all-purpose flour
   1/4 teaspoon salt
   4 large eggs

For the Pastry Cream:

6. 2 cups whole milk

   1/2 cup granulated sugar
   1/4 cup cornstarch
   4 large egg yolks
   2 teaspoons vanilla extract

For the Chocolate Glaze:

11. 4 ounces (about 1/2 cup) dark chocolate, chopped

    1/2 cup heavy cream
    1 tablespoon unsalted butter

Instructions:

1. Prepare the Choux Pastry:

   - In a medium saucepan, bring water and butter to a boil. Add flour and salt, stirring continuously until the mixture forms a ball and pulls away from the sides of the pan.
   - Remove from heat and let it cool for a couple of minutes.

- Add eggs one at a time, beating well after each addition, until you have a smooth, glossy dough.

2. Pipe the Éclair Shells:

- Preheat your oven to 425°F (220°C).
- Transfer the choux pastry into a piping bag fitted with a large round tip.
- Pipe 4-inch long éclair shapes onto a baking sheet lined with parchment paper.
- Bake for 15 minutes at 425°F, then reduce the temperature to 375°F (190°C) and bake for an additional 15-20 minutes or until golden brown and puffed.

3. Prepare the Pastry Cream:

- In a saucepan, heat the milk until it just begins to boil.
- In a bowl, whisk together sugar, cornstarch, and egg yolks until well combined.
- Slowly pour the hot milk into the egg mixture while continuously whisking.
- Return the mixture to the saucepan and cook over medium heat, stirring constantly, until it thickens.
- Remove from heat, stir in vanilla extract, and let it cool.

4. Fill the Éclairs:

- Once the éclair shells are cooled, cut them in half horizontally.
- Fill a piping bag with the cooled pastry cream and pipe it onto the bottom half of each éclair.

5. Prepare the Chocolate Glaze:

- In a heatproof bowl, combine the chopped chocolate, heavy cream, and butter.
- Microwave in short bursts or use a double boiler until the chocolate is melted and the mixture is smooth.

6. Glaze the Éclairs:

- Dip the top half of each filled éclair into the chocolate glaze.
- Allow the chocolate to set slightly before serving.

7. Serve:

- Arrange the éclairs on a serving platter and enjoy!

These homemade éclairs are a delightful treat, with a perfect balance of crisp pastry, creamy fil

Tarte Tatin

Ingredients:

For the Caramel:

>1 cup granulated sugar
>1/4 cup water
>1/2 cup unsalted butter, cut into small pieces

For the Apple Filling:

4. 6-8 large apples (such as Granny Smith), peeled, cored, and halved

>1 tablespoon lemon juice
>1/2 teaspoon ground cinnamon (optional)

For the Pastry:

7. 1 sheet of puff pastry (store-bought or homemade), thawed if frozen

Instructions:

1. Preheat the Oven:

- Preheat your oven to 375°F (190°C).

2. Make the Caramel:

- In a 9 or 10-inch ovenproof skillet or Tarte Tatin pan, combine sugar and water over medium heat.
- Swirl the pan occasionally until the sugar dissolves and turns a deep amber color.
- Remove from heat and whisk in the butter until smooth.

3. Arrange the Apples:

- Arrange the apple halves, rounded side down, in a circular pattern over the caramel in the skillet.
- Sprinkle lemon juice and cinnamon over the apples.

4. Cook on the Stovetop:

    - Place the skillet back on the stove over medium heat.
    - Cook for about 15-20 minutes, allowing the apples to caramelize in the butter and sugar. Occasionally spoon the caramel over the apples.

5. Prepare the Puff Pastry:

    - Roll out the puff pastry on a lightly floured surface to a size slightly larger than the skillet.

6. Assemble the Tarte Tatin:

    - Place the puff pastry over the caramelized apples, tucking in the edges around the apples.
    - Cut a few small slits in the pastry to allow steam to escape.

7. Bake:

    - Transfer the skillet to the preheated oven and bake for 20-25 minutes or until the pastry is golden brown and puffed.

8. Flip and Serve:

    - Remove the skillet from the oven and let it cool for a couple of minutes.
    - Place a serving plate over the skillet and carefully flip the Tarte Tatin onto the plate.

9. Serve:

    - Serve the Tarte Tatin warm, either on its own or with a dollop of whipped cream or a scoop of vanilla ice cream.

Enjoy the irresistible flavors of this classic French upside-down apple tart!

Macarons

Ingredients:

For the Macaron Shells:

- 1 cup (100g) almond flour
- 1 3/4 cups (210g) powdered sugar
- 3 large egg whites, at room temperature
- 1/4 cup (50g) granulated sugar
- 1/2 teaspoon vanilla extract (optional)
- Gel food coloring (optional)

For the Filling:

7. 1/2 cup (120g) unsalted butter, softened

- 1 cup (120g) powdered sugar
- 1-2 teaspoons flavored extract (e.g., vanilla, almond, or any flavor of your choice)
- Jam, ganache, or curd for filling (optional)

Instructions:

1. Prepare Baking Sheets:

- Line two baking sheets with parchment paper or silicone baking mats.

2. Make Almond Mixture:

- In a food processor, combine almond flour and powdered sugar. Pulse until fine and well combined. Sieve the mixture to remove any lumps.

3. Whip Egg Whites:

- In a clean, dry bowl, beat the egg whites until foamy. Gradually add granulated sugar, continuing to beat until stiff peaks form. Add vanilla extract and food coloring, if using, and gently fold to combine.

4. Macaronage:

- Carefully fold the almond mixture into the whipped egg whites using a spatula until the batter is smooth and glossy. This step is called macaronage.

5. Pipe Macarons:

- Transfer the batter into a piping bag fitted with a round tip. Pipe small rounds onto the prepared baking sheets, leaving space between each.

6. Resting Time:

- Let the piped macarons sit at room temperature for about 30 minutes to an hour. This forms a skin on the surface.

7. Preheat and Bake:

- Preheat your oven to 300°F (150°C).
- Bake the macarons for 15-20 minutes or until they have developed feet and are set but not browned.

8. Cool Completely:

- Allow the macarons to cool completely on the baking sheets before attempting to remove them.

9. Prepare Filling:

- While the macarons are cooling, prepare the filling. Beat together the softened butter, powdered sugar, and flavored extract until smooth.

10. Fill the Macarons:

- Pair up the cooled macaron shells based on size. Pipe or spoon a small amount of filling onto the flat side of one shell and sandwich it with another.

11. Age (Optional):

- If possible, age the filled macarons in the refrigerator for 24 hours before serving. This allows the flavors to meld.

12. Serve:

- Bring the macarons to room temperature before serving. Enjoy the delicate and flavorful French macarons!

Note: Macarons can be a bit tricky, and practice improves results. Factors like humidity, egg whites' stiffness, and oven temperature can affect the outcome.

Palmiers

Ingredients:

    1 sheet puff pastry (store-bought or homemade)
    1 cup granulated sugar
    1/2 teaspoon ground cinnamon (optional)

Instructions:

1. Preheat Oven:

- Preheat your oven to 400°F (200°C).

2. Prepare Puff Pastry:

- If using store-bought puff pastry, thaw it according to the package instructions. If making your own, roll it out into a rectangle on a lightly floured surface.

3. Spread Sugar Mixture:

- In a small bowl, combine the granulated sugar and ground cinnamon if using.
- Sprinkle half of the sugar mixture evenly over your rolled-out puff pastry.

4. Fold the Edges:

- Starting from one of the longer edges, fold each side of the puff pastry towards the center so they meet in the middle.

5. Sprinkle More Sugar:

- Sprinkle the remaining sugar mixture over the folded pastry.

6. Fold Again:

- Fold the pastry in half along the centerline, creating a double-layered log.

7. Slice the Palmiers:

    - Using a sharp knife, cut the log into slices about 1/2-inch thick.

8. Arrange on Baking Sheet:

    - Place the palmier slices on a baking sheet lined with parchment paper, leaving some space between each.

9. Bake:

    - Bake in the preheated oven for about 10-12 minutes or until the palmiers are golden brown and caramelized.

10. Cool:

    - Allow the palmiers to cool on the baking sheet for a few minutes, then transfer them to a wire rack to cool completely.

11. Serve:

    - Serve the palmiers as a delightful sweet treat with your favorite beverage.

Palmiers, also known as elephant ears or puff pastry hearts, are a simple yet elegant French pastry. They are perfect for a quick and delicious dessert or as a sweet snack with your afternoon tea or coffee.

Madeleines

Ingredients:

- 2/3 cup (150g) unsalted butter, melted and cooled
- 1 cup (125g) all-purpose flour
- 1/2 teaspoon baking powder
- 1/4 teaspoon salt
- 3 large eggs, room temperature
- 2/3 cup (130g) granulated sugar
- 1 teaspoon vanilla extract
- Zest of 1 lemon (optional, for flavor)
- Powdered sugar, for dusting (optional)

Instructions:

1. Prepare Madeleine Pans:

   - Grease the madeleine pans with butter or cooking spray. Dust with a little flour, tapping out any excess.

2. Melt and Cool Butter:

   - Melt the butter in a saucepan or microwave and let it cool to room temperature.

3. Sift Dry Ingredients:

   - In a bowl, sift together the flour, baking powder, and salt. Set aside.

4. Whip Eggs and Sugar:

   - In a large bowl, using an electric mixer, beat the eggs and granulated sugar until thick and pale. This may take about 5 minutes.

5. Add Flavorings:

   - Add the vanilla extract and lemon zest (if using) to the egg-sugar mixture. Mix until combined.

6. Fold in Dry Ingredients:

- Gently fold the sifted dry ingredients into the egg-sugar mixture until just combined.

7. Incorporate Melted Butter:

    - Pour the cooled melted butter over the batter and fold it in until smooth.

8. Chill the Batter:

    - Cover the batter and refrigerate for at least 1 hour or overnight. This helps in achieving the characteristic hump on the madeleines.

9. Preheat Oven:

    - Preheat your oven to 375°F (190°C).

10. Fill the Madeleine Pans:

    - Spoon the chilled batter into the prepared madeleine pans, filling each mold about 3/4 full.

11. Bake:

    - Bake in the preheated oven for 10-12 minutes or until the madeleines are golden around the edges and have a slight hump in the center.

12. Cool and Dust (Optional):

    - Allow the madeleines to cool in the pans for a few minutes before transferring them to a wire rack to cool completely.
    - Dust with powdered sugar before serving, if desired.

13. Serve:

    - Serve the madeleines with a cup of tea or coffee, and enjoy the delicate, shell-shaped treats.

These French madeleines are best when fresh, with a slightly crispy exterior and a soft, spongy interior. They are perfect for serving at tea time or as a delightful snack.

Financiers

Ingredients:

    1 cup (225g) unsalted butter
    1 cup (100g) almond flour
    1 1/2 cups (180g) powdered sugar
    1/2 cup (60g) all-purpose flour
    1/2 teaspoon baking powder
    5 egg whites
    1 teaspoon vanilla extract
    Pinch of salt
    Sliced almonds for decoration (optional)

Instructions:

1. Brown the Butter:

- In a saucepan, melt the butter over medium heat. Continue cooking until it turns a light brown color, giving it a nutty aroma. Remove from heat and let it cool to room temperature.

2. Preheat Oven:

- Preheat your oven to 375°F (190°C). Grease and flour your financier molds or mini-muffin tins.

3. Mix Dry Ingredients:

- In a bowl, whisk together almond flour, powdered sugar, all-purpose flour, baking powder, and a pinch of salt.

4. Whip Egg Whites:

- In another bowl, whisk the egg whites until they are frothy but not stiff.

5. Combine Ingredients:

- Gently fold the dry ingredients into the egg whites, being careful not to deflate them.
- Add the cooled browned butter and vanilla extract, continuing to fold until you have a smooth batter.

6. Fill Molds:

- Pour the batter into the prepared molds, filling each about 2/3 full.

7. Decorate (Optional):

- If desired, sprinkle sliced almonds on top of each financier for added texture.

8. Bake:

- Bake in the preheated oven for approximately 15-18 minutes or until the financiers are golden brown around the edges and a toothpick inserted into the center comes out clean.

9. Cool:

- Allow the financiers to cool in the molds for a few minutes before transferring them to a wire rack to cool completely.

10. Serve:

- Serve the financiers with a dusting of powdered sugar, if desired. They are delicious with tea or coffee.

Financiers are small, almond-flavored cakes with a delightful nutty taste. These petite treats are not only delicious but also elegant, making them perfect for a special occasion or an afternoon tea.

Chausson aux Pommes (Apple Turnovers)

Ingredients:

For the Apple Filling:

    3 large apples (such as Granny Smith), peeled, cored, and diced
    1/4 cup (50g) granulated sugar
    1/2 teaspoon ground cinnamon
    1 tablespoon lemon juice
    2 tablespoons unsalted butter

For the Pastry:

6. 1 package (about 17.3 ounces or 2 sheets) puff pastry, thawed if frozen

    Flour for dusting
    1 egg, beaten (for egg wash)
    Powdered sugar for dusting (optional)

Instructions:

1. Prepare the Apple Filling:

- In a saucepan, melt butter over medium heat. Add diced apples, sugar, cinnamon, and lemon juice. Cook until the apples are tender, about 5-7 minutes. Set aside to cool.

2. Preheat Oven:

- Preheat your oven to 375°F (190°C). Line a baking sheet with parchment paper.

3. Roll Out the Puff Pastry:

- On a lightly floured surface, roll out the puff pastry into a large rectangle. If using pre-rolled sheets, make sure they are evenly rolled.

4. Cut Pastry into Squares:

- Cut the puff pastry into squares of your desired size. Typically, 4 to 6 inches per side works well.

5. Fill and Fold:

    - Place a spoonful of the cooled apple filling in the center of each pastry square.
    - Fold the pastry over the filling, creating a triangle or rectangle shape. Press the edges to seal.

6. Seal Edges:

    - Use a fork to crimp the edges, sealing the turnovers tightly.

7. Egg Wash:

    - Brush each turnover with beaten egg for a golden finish during baking.

8. Bake:

    - Place the turnovers on the prepared baking sheet and bake in the preheated oven for 15-20 minutes or until they are puffed and golden brown.

9. Cool:

    - Allow the apple turnovers to cool on a wire rack.

10. Dust with Powdered Sugar (Optional):

    - Dust with powdered sugar before serving if desired.

11. Serve:

    - Serve the Chausson aux Pommes warm or at room temperature. Enjoy as a delicious dessert or sweet treat with a cup of tea or coffee.

These apple turnovers are a classic French pastry, featuring flaky puff pastry filled with sweet and spiced apples. They're a delightful treat that's perfect for breakfast or dessert.

Pâte à Choux

Ingredients:

> 1 cup water
> 1/2 cup (1 stick) unsalted butter
> 1 cup all-purpose flour
> 4 large eggs
> 1/4 teaspoon salt
> 1 tablespoon granulated sugar (for sweet applications, optional)

Instructions:

1. Preheat Oven:

- Preheat your oven to 425°F (220°C) for savory applications or 375°F (190°C) for sweet applications.

2. Prepare Baking Sheets:

- Line baking sheets with parchment paper or silicone baking mats.

3. Make the Dough:

- In a medium saucepan, combine water, butter, salt, and sugar (if making sweet pâte à choux). Heat over medium-high heat until the mixture comes to a boil and the butter is melted.

4. Add Flour:

- Reduce the heat to low, add the flour all at once, and stir vigorously with a wooden spoon until the mixture forms a smooth ball and pulls away from the sides of the pan.

5. Cool Slightly:

- Remove the pan from the heat and let the mixture cool for a couple of minutes.

6. Add Eggs:

    - Add the eggs one at a time, beating well after each addition. The dough will initially appear lumpy, but it will become smooth and glossy.

7. Check Consistency:

    - The dough should have a smooth, shiny, and thick consistency. It should be able to hold its shape but still be pipeable.

8. Pipe or Spoon onto Baking Sheets:

    - Transfer the dough to a piping bag fitted with a plain round tip or use two spoons to drop mounds onto the prepared baking sheets. For éclairs or cream puffs, pipe fingers or circles.

9. Bake:

    - Bake in the preheated oven until golden brown and puffed up. This typically takes 15-20 minutes, depending on the size of the pastries.

10. Cool:

    - Allow the baked pâte à choux to cool on a wire rack.

11. Fill or Top:

    - Once cooled, you can fill the pâte à choux with pastry cream, whipped cream, ice cream, or savory fillings. For cream puffs or profiteroles, you can cut them in half horizontally and fill them.

12. Serve:

- Serve the filled or topped pastries and enjoy the light and airy texture of pâte à choux.

Pâte à Choux is a versatile pastry dough used in a variety of French pastries like éclairs, cream puffs, profiteroles, and more. It's the foundation for many delicious desserts and can be customized for both sweet and savory applications.

Profiteroles

Ingredients:

For the Pâte à Choux:

    1 cup water
    1/2 cup (1 stick) unsalted butter
    1 cup all-purpose flour
    4 large eggs
    1/4 teaspoon salt
    1 tablespoon granulated sugar (optional)

For the Filling:

7. 2 cups vanilla ice cream or pastry cream

For the Chocolate Sauce:

8. 4 ounces (about 1/2 cup) dark chocolate, finely chopped

    1/2 cup heavy cream
    2 tablespoons unsalted butter
    1 tablespoon powdered sugar (optional)

Instructions:

1. Make the Pâte à Choux:

- Follow the instructions for making Pâte à Choux from the previous recipe.

2. Pipe and Bake:

- Preheat your oven to 375°F (190°C).
- Pipe small mounds of Pâte à Choux onto a baking sheet lined with parchment paper, leaving space between each.
- Bake in the preheated oven for 15-20 minutes or until the profiteroles are golden brown and puffed.

3. Cool:

- Allow the profiteroles to cool completely on a wire rack.

4. Prepare the Filling:

    - Once cooled, cut the profiteroles in half horizontally.
    - Fill each profiterole with a scoop of vanilla ice cream or pastry cream.

5. Make Chocolate Sauce:

    - In a heatproof bowl, combine the chopped dark chocolate, heavy cream, and butter.
    - Melt the ingredients together using a double boiler or by microwaving in short bursts.
    - Stir in powdered sugar if desired for sweetness.

6. Assemble:

    - Drizzle the warm chocolate sauce over the filled profiteroles.

7. Serve:

    - Serve the profiteroles immediately while the chocolate sauce is still warm.

Profiteroles are delightful cream puffs filled with ice cream or pastry cream and topped with a decadent chocolate sauce. They make for an elegant and impressive dessert for special occasions or any sweet craving.

Galette des Rois

Ingredients:

For the Almond Filling:

    1 cup almond flour
    1/2 cup granulated sugar
    1/2 cup unsalted butter, softened
    2 large eggs
    1 teaspoon vanilla extract
    1 tablespoon all-purpose flour

For the Puff Pastry:

7. 2 sheets (about 17.3 ounces) of puff pastry, thawed if frozen

    1 egg yolk (for egg wash)

For Decoration (Optional):

9. Powdered sugar

    Colored sugar or sprinkles

Instructions:

1. Prepare the Almond Filling:

   - In a bowl, combine almond flour, granulated sugar, softened butter, eggs, vanilla extract, and all-purpose flour. Mix until well combined and smooth.

2. Roll Out the Puff Pastry:

   - Roll out each sheet of puff pastry into a circle on a lightly floured surface. Make sure one of the circles is slightly larger, as it will be the base.

3. Place the Filling:

   - Place the smaller puff pastry circle on a baking sheet lined with parchment paper.

- Spread the almond filling evenly over the center of the pastry, leaving a border around the edges.

4. Add the Bean or Figurine (Optional):

    - Tradition dictates that a small figurine or bean be hidden in the filling. Place it somewhere in the almond mixture.

5. Top with the Second Puff Pastry:

    - Lay the larger puff pastry circle over the almond filling.
    - Press the edges together to seal the galette.

6. Decorate and Score:

    - If desired, use a knife to score decorative patterns on the top of the galette.
    - Brush the top with beaten egg yolk for a golden finish.

7. Chill:

    - Chill the assembled galette in the refrigerator for at least 30 minutes.

8. Preheat Oven:

    - Preheat your oven to 375°F (190°C).

9. Bake:

    - Bake the galette in the preheated oven for 25-30 minutes or until golden brown and puffed.

10. Cool and Decorate:

    - Allow the galette to cool on a wire rack. Once cooled, you can dust it with powdered sugar and decorate with colored sugar or sprinkles.

11. Serve:

    - Slice and serve the Galette des Rois. The person who finds the hidden bean or figurine in their slice is crowned "king" or "queen" for the day.

The Galette des Rois is a traditional French pastry often enjoyed during the Epiphany season. It features a buttery puff pastry filled with a delicious almond cream filling, and it's a delightful treat to share with family and friends.

Pithiviers

Ingredients:

For the Puff Pastry:

    2 sheets of store-bought puff pastry (or homemade if preferred)
    1 egg (for egg wash)

For the Almond Filling:

3. 1 cup (100g) almond flour

    2/3 cup (135g) granulated sugar
    1/2 cup (115g) unsalted butter, softened
    2 large eggs
    1 teaspoon almond extract
    1 tablespoon all-purpose flour
    1 dry fava bean or small figurine (to hide in the filling)

For the Glaze (Optional):

10. 1/2 cup (60g) powdered sugar

    1-2 tablespoons water
    Sliced almonds for decoration (optional)

Instructions:

1. Preheat Oven:

- Preheat your oven to 400°F (200°C).

2. Prepare Puff Pastry:

- Roll out one sheet of puff pastry on a lightly floured surface. Place it on a baking sheet lined with parchment paper.

3. Make Almond Filling:

- In a bowl, combine almond flour, granulated sugar, softened butter, eggs, almond extract, and all-purpose flour. Mix until smooth.

4. Assemble:

    - Spread the almond filling evenly over the rolled-out puff pastry, leaving a border around the edges.
    - If using, place a dry fava bean or small figurine somewhere in the filling.

5. Cover with Second Puff Pastry:

    - Roll out the second sheet of puff pastry and place it on top of the almond filling. Press the edges to seal.

6. Create Decorative Pattern:

    - Use a knife to create a decorative pattern on the top of the galette, such as a crisscross or spirals. Be careful not to cut through the pastry.

7. Egg Wash:

    - Beat an egg and brush it over the top of the galette for a golden finish.

8. Bake:

    - Bake in the preheated oven for 20-25 minutes or until the galette is golden brown and puffed.

9. Make Glaze (Optional):

    - If desired, mix powdered sugar with water to create a glaze. Drizzle it over the galette and sprinkle with sliced almonds.

10. Serve:

    - Allow the galette to cool slightly before serving. Tradition dictates that the person who finds the hidden fava bean or figurine in their slice is crowned the king or queen.

Note:

- It's important to hide the fava bean or figurine well within the filling to make finding it a surprise for one lucky person.

Galette des Rois is a traditional French pastry enjoyed during the Epiphany season. It features a delicious almond filling enclosed in flaky puff pastry, making it a delightful treat for celebrations.

Mille-Feuille

Ingredients:

For the Puff Pastry:

> 2 sheets of store-bought puff pastry (or homemade, if preferred)
> Confectioners' sugar for dusting

For the Pastry Cream:

3. 2 cups whole milk

> 1 vanilla bean or 1 teaspoon vanilla extract
> 6 large egg yolks
> 1 cup granulated sugar
> 1/3 cup cornstarch
> 2 tablespoons unsalted butter

For the Glaze:

9. 1 cup confectioners' sugar

> 2 tablespoons water
> 1 teaspoon vanilla extract

Instructions:

1. Preheat Oven:

- Preheat your oven to 400°F (200°C).

2. Prepare Puff Pastry:

- Roll out each sheet of puff pastry on a lightly floured surface. Place them on baking sheets lined with parchment paper.
- Prick the surface of the pastry with a fork to prevent excessive rising.

3. Bake Puff Pastry:

- Bake in the preheated oven for 15-20 minutes or until golden brown and puffed. Keep an eye on them to avoid over-browning.
- Remove from the oven and let them cool completely.

4. Make Pastry Cream:

    - In a saucepan, heat the milk over medium heat. If using a vanilla bean, split it lengthwise, scrape the seeds, and add both seeds and pod to the milk. Bring to a simmer and then remove from heat.
    - In a bowl, whisk together egg yolks, sugar, and cornstarch until well combined.
    - Slowly pour the hot milk into the egg mixture while continuously whisking.
    - Return the mixture to the saucepan and cook over medium heat, stirring constantly, until it thickens.
    - Remove from heat, discard the vanilla pod if used, and stir in butter. Let it cool.

5. Assemble Mille-Feuille:

    - Place one sheet of baked puff pastry on a serving platter. Spread a layer of pastry cream evenly over the pastry.
    - Place the second sheet of puff pastry on top and press gently.

6. Make Glaze:

    - In a bowl, whisk together confectioners' sugar, water, and vanilla extract to create a glaze.

7. Glaze the Mille-Feuille:

    - Pour the glaze over the top of the assembled mille-feuille, spreading it evenly with a spatula.

8. Chill:

    - Refrigerate the mille-feuille for at least 1-2 hours to allow the layers to set.

9. Slice and Serve:

    - Once chilled, use a sharp knife to slice the mille-feuille into portions.
    - Dust the top with confectioners' sugar before serving if desired.

Mille-Feuille, also known as Napoleon, is a classic French pastry with layers of crispy puff pastry and luscious pastry cream. It's a visually stunning and delicious dessert, perfect for special occasions.

Opera Cake

Ingredients:

For the Joconde Sponge:

    1 cup almond flour
    1 cup powdered sugar
    3 large eggs
    3 large egg whites
    1/4 cup granulated sugar
    1/3 cup all-purpose flour
    2 tablespoons unsalted butter, melted

For the Coffee Syrup:

8. 1/2 cup strong brewed coffee, cooled

    2 tablespoons sugar
    2 tablespoons coffee liqueur (optional)

For the Coffee Buttercream:

11. 1 cup unsalted butter, softened

    1 cup powdered sugar
    2 teaspoons instant coffee powder, dissolved in 1 tablespoon hot water
    1 teaspoon vanilla extract

For the Chocolate Ganache:

15. 4 ounces dark chocolate, finely chopped

    1/2 cup heavy cream

Instructions:

1. Preheat Oven:

   - Preheat your oven to 425°F (220°C). Grease and line a 9x13-inch baking sheet with parchment paper.

2. Make Joconde Sponge:

   - In a bowl, combine almond flour and powdered sugar. Add the whole eggs and mix until smooth.
   - In a separate bowl, whip the egg whites until soft peaks form. Gradually add granulated sugar and continue whipping until stiff peaks form.
   - Gently fold the whipped egg whites into the almond mixture. Add the melted butter and sifted flour, folding until just combined.
   - Spread the batter evenly onto the prepared baking sheet and bake for 8-10 minutes or until the sponge is lightly golden and springs back when touched.
   - Let it cool.

3. Prepare Coffee Syrup:

   - In a small saucepan, combine brewed coffee and sugar. Bring to a simmer, stirring until the sugar dissolves. Remove from heat, add coffee liqueur if using, and let it cool.

4. Make Coffee Buttercream:

   - In a bowl, beat the softened butter until creamy. Add powdered sugar, dissolved instant coffee, and vanilla extract. Beat until smooth and fluffy.

5. Assemble Opera Cake:

   - Cut the cooled Joconde sponge into three equal rectangles.
   - Place one layer in the bottom of a lined 9x9-inch square cake pan.
   - Brush the sponge with coffee syrup.
   - Spread half of the coffee buttercream over the sponge.
   - Place the second layer of sponge on top and repeat the process.
   - Top with the third layer of sponge and brush with coffee syrup.

6. Prepare Chocolate Ganache:

    - In a heatproof bowl, melt the chopped chocolate with the heavy cream over a double boiler or in the microwave. Stir until smooth.

7. Cover with Chocolate Ganache:

    - Pour the chocolate ganache over the top layer of the cake, spreading it evenly.

8. Chill:

    - Refrigerate the opera cake for at least 4 hours or overnight to allow the layers to set.

9. Slice and Serve:

    - Once chilled, use a sharp knife dipped in hot water to slice the opera cake into portions. Clean the knife between each cut for neat slices.
    - Serve and enjoy this elegant and decadent French dessert.

The Opera Cake is a sophisticated layered dessert with almond sponge, coffee syrup, coffee buttercream, and a smooth chocolate ganache. It's a true delight for coffee and chocolate lovers alike.

Brioche

Ingredients:

For the Brioche Dough:

    4 cups (500g) all-purpose flour
    1/4 cup (50g) granulated sugar
    1 teaspoon salt
    1 tablespoon active dry yeast
    1/2 cup (120ml) warm milk
    4 large eggs, room temperature
    1 cup (225g) unsalted butter, softened

For the Egg Wash:

8. 1 egg, beaten

    1 tablespoon milk

Instructions:

1. Activate Yeast:

- In a small bowl, combine warm milk and a pinch of sugar. Sprinkle the active dry yeast over the milk and let it sit for about 5-10 minutes until it becomes frothy.

2. Mix Dry Ingredients:

- In a large mixing bowl, whisk together the flour, sugar, and salt.

3. Make Dough:

- Create a well in the center of the dry ingredients. Pour in the frothy yeast mixture and add the eggs.
- Mix the ingredients together to form a sticky dough.

4. Incorporate Butter:

   - Gradually add the softened butter, one tablespoon at a time, kneading continuously until the dough becomes smooth and elastic. This can take about 10-15 minutes.

5. First Rise:

   - Place the dough in a lightly greased bowl, cover it with a clean kitchen towel, and let it rise in a warm place for 1-2 hours or until it has doubled in size.

6. Punch Down:

   - Gently punch down the risen dough to release excess air.

7. Shape the Brioche:

   - Divide the dough into two equal portions. Shape each portion into a loaf or braid, depending on your preference. Place the shaped dough in greased loaf pans or on a baking sheet.

8. Second Rise:

   - Cover the shaped dough with a kitchen towel and let it rise for an additional 1-2 hours until it doubles in size.

9. Preheat Oven:

   - Preheat your oven to 375°F (190°C).

10. Egg Wash:

    - In a small bowl, whisk together the beaten egg and milk. Brush the egg wash over the top of the shaped brioche.

11. Bake:

- Bake in the preheated oven for 25-30 minutes or until the brioche is golden brown and sounds hollow when tapped on the bottom.

12. Cool:

- Allow the brioche to cool in the pans for a few minutes before transferring them to a wire rack to cool completely.

13. Serve:

- Slice and serve the brioche on its own or with your favorite spread. Enjoy the buttery, rich flavor and tender texture of this classic French bread.

Brioche is a versatile and delicious bread that can be enjoyed for breakfast or as a sweet treat. Whether served plain, with butter, or used in French toast or bread pudding, brioche is sure to become a favorite in your kitchen.

Tarte aux Fruits (Fruit Tart)

Ingredients:

For the Tart Shell:

    1 1/4 cups (160g) all-purpose flour
    1/2 cup (60g) powdered sugar
    1/4 teaspoon salt
    1/2 cup (115g) unsalted butter, cold and cut into small pieces
    1 large egg yolk
    1-2 tablespoons cold water

For the Pastry Cream:

7. 1 1/2 cups (360ml) whole milk

    1/2 cup (100g) granulated sugar
    4 large egg yolks
    1/4 cup (30g) cornstarch
    1 teaspoon vanilla extract

For Topping:

12. Assorted fresh fruits (strawberries, kiwi, blueberries, raspberries, etc.)

    Apricot or fruit glaze for brushing (optional)

Instructions:

1. Prepare Tart Shell:

- In a food processor, pulse together the flour, powdered sugar, and salt. Add the cold butter and pulse until the mixture resembles coarse crumbs.
- In a small bowl, whisk together the egg yolk and 1 tablespoon of cold water. Add it to the flour-butter mixture and pulse until the dough comes together. If needed, add an extra tablespoon of water.

- Turn the dough onto a lightly floured surface and knead it just until it comes together. Shape it into a disk, wrap it in plastic wrap, and refrigerate for at least 1 hour.

2. Roll and Bake the Tart Shell:

- Preheat your oven to 375°F (190°C).
- Roll out the chilled dough on a floured surface to fit your tart pan. Press the dough into the pan, trimming any excess.
- Prick the bottom of the tart shell with a fork, line it with parchment paper, and fill with pie weights or dried beans.
- Bake for 15 minutes. Remove the weights and parchment paper, and bake for an additional 10-15 minutes or until the crust is golden brown. Allow it to cool completely.

3. Make Pastry Cream:

- In a saucepan, heat the milk until it is just about to boil.
- In a separate bowl, whisk together the sugar, egg yolks, and cornstarch until well combined.
- Slowly pour the hot milk into the egg mixture while whisking continuously.
- Pour the mixture back into the saucepan and cook over medium heat, stirring constantly, until it thickens.
- Remove from heat, stir in the vanilla extract, and let it cool.

4. Assemble the Tart:

- Spread the cooled pastry cream over the baked and cooled tart shell.
- Arrange fresh fruits on top of the pastry cream in an attractive pattern.

5. Optional Glaze:

- If desired, melt apricot or fruit glaze and brush it over the top of the fruits to give them a shiny appearance.

6. Chill and Serve:

- Refrigerate the tart for at least 1-2 hours before serving to allow the flavors to meld.
- Slice and serve the delicious Tarte aux Fruits. Enjoy the combination of the buttery crust, creamy pastry cream, and fresh, vibrant fruits!

This Fruit Tart is a delightful dessert that showcases the beauty and flavors of seasonal fruits. It's perfect for special occasions or any time you want to impress with a visually stunning and delicious treat.

Kouign-Amann

Ingredients:

For the Dough:

    2 1/4 teaspoons (1 packet) active dry yeast
    1 1/4 cups warm water
    3 1/2 cups all-purpose flour, plus extra for dusting
    1 teaspoon salt
    1 cup unsalted butter, cold

For the Filling:

6. 1 cup granulated sugar, plus extra for rolling

    Additional 1/2 cup unsalted butter, softened

Instructions:

1. Activate Yeast:

- In a bowl, combine the active dry yeast with warm water. Let it sit for about 5-10 minutes until it becomes frothy.

2. Make Dough:

- In a large mixing bowl, combine the flour and salt. Add the frothy yeast mixture and mix until a dough forms.
- Knead the dough on a floured surface for about 5-7 minutes or until it becomes smooth.

3. Roll Out Dough:

- Roll out the dough into a large rectangle on a floured surface.

4. Add Butter:

   - Cut the cold butter into thin slices and arrange them evenly over two-thirds of the dough.

5. Fold the Dough:

   - Fold the remaining third of the dough over the butter-covered portion, then fold the other end over the top, creating a trifold.

6. Chill:

   - Wrap the dough in plastic wrap and refrigerate for at least 30 minutes.

7. Roll and Fold:

   - Roll out the chilled dough again into a rectangle and perform a trifold. Repeat this process 3-4 times, allowing the dough to chill between each fold.

8. Preheat Oven:

   - Preheat your oven to 375°F (190°C).

9. Prepare Pan:

   - Generously butter a muffin tin or individual ramekins.

10. Make Sugar Filling:

    - In a bowl, combine 1 cup of granulated sugar. Spread an additional 1/2 cup of softened butter over the rolled-out dough and sprinkle it with sugar.

11. Cut and Place in Pans:

    - Cut the dough into squares and place each square into the buttered and sugared muffin tin or ramekins.

12. Bake:

- Bake in the preheated oven for about 25-30 minutes or until the Kouign-Amann is golden brown and caramelized.

13. Cool:

- Allow the Kouign-Amann to cool in the pan for a few minutes before transferring them to a wire rack.

14. Serve:

- Serve the Kouign-Amann warm or at room temperature. Enjoy the delicious layers of buttery, caramelized goodness!

Kouign-Amann is a decadent Breton pastry known for its crispy, caramelized layers.

While it requires a bit of effort, the result is a delightful treat that's well worth it!

Paris-Brest

Ingredients:

For the Choux Pastry:

    1/2 cup water
    1/2 cup whole milk
    1/2 cup (1 stick) unsalted butter
    1 tablespoon granulated sugar
    1/4 teaspoon salt
    1 cup all-purpose flour
    4 large eggs

For the Praline Cream:

8. 1 cup whole milk

    4 large egg yolks
    1/2 cup granulated sugar
    1/4 cup cornstarch
    1 teaspoon vanilla extract
    1 cup praline paste

For the Assembly:

14. Sliced almonds, toasted (for garnish)

    Powdered sugar (for dusting)

Instructions:

1. Preheat Oven:

- Preheat your oven to 425°F (220°C). Line a baking sheet with parchment paper.

2. Make Choux Pastry:

- In a saucepan, combine water, milk, butter, sugar, and salt. Bring to a boil.

- Add the flour all at once and stir vigorously with a wooden spoon until the mixture forms a smooth ball.
- Transfer the dough to a mixing bowl and let it cool for a few minutes.
- Add the eggs one at a time, beating well after each addition, until the dough is smooth and glossy.

3. Pipe and Bake:

- Pipe a ring of choux pastry on the prepared baking sheet using a large round tip or a pastry bag. You can also use a circular mold to guide the shape.
- Bake in the preheated oven for 20-25 minutes or until the pastry is golden brown and puffed.
- Allow it to cool completely.

4. Make Praline Cream:

- In a saucepan, heat the milk until it's hot but not boiling.
- In a bowl, whisk together egg yolks, sugar, cornstarch, and vanilla extract until well combined.
- Slowly pour the hot milk into the egg mixture, whisking constantly.
- Return the mixture to the saucepan and cook over medium heat, stirring continuously until it thickens.
- Remove from heat, stir in praline paste until smooth, and let it cool.

5. Assemble Paris-Brest:

- Slice the choux pastry ring horizontally.
- Fill the bottom half with the praline cream.
- Place the top half back on and press gently.
- Garnish with toasted sliced almonds and dust with powdered sugar.

6. Serve:

- Slice and serve the Paris-Brest. Enjoy the delightful combination of crisp choux pastry and praline-flavored cream.

Paris-Brest is a classic French pastry named after the Paris to Brest bicycle race. It features a ring of choux pastry filled with praline cream, creating a delicious and visually appealing dessert.

Religieuse

Ingredients:

For the Choux Pastry:

    1/2 cup water
    1/2 cup whole milk
    1/2 cup (1 stick) unsalted butter
    1 tablespoon granulated sugar
    1/4 teaspoon salt
    1 cup all-purpose flour
    4 large eggs

For the Pastry Cream:

8. 1 cup whole milk

    4 large egg yolks
    1/2 cup granulated sugar
    1/4 cup cornstarch
    1 teaspoon vanilla extract

For the Chocolate Glaze:

13. 4 ounces dark chocolate, finely chopped

    1/2 cup heavy cream
    1 tablespoon unsalted butter

Instructions:

1. Preheat Oven:

- Preheat your oven to 425°F (220°C). Line a baking sheet with parchment paper.

2. Make Choux Pastry:

- In a saucepan, combine water, milk, butter, sugar, and salt. Bring to a boil.
- Add the flour all at once and stir vigorously with a wooden spoon until the mixture forms a smooth ball.
- Transfer the dough to a mixing bowl and let it cool for a few minutes.
- Add the eggs one at a time, beating well after each addition, until the dough is smooth and glossy.

3. Pipe and Bake:

- Pipe small rounds of choux pastry onto the prepared baking sheet using a pastry bag or two spoons.
- Bake in the preheated oven for 20-25 minutes or until the pastries are golden brown and puffed.
- Allow them to cool completely.

4. Make Pastry Cream:

- In a saucepan, heat the milk until hot but not boiling.
- In a bowl, whisk together egg yolks, sugar, cornstarch, and vanilla extract until well combined.
- Slowly pour the hot milk into the egg mixture, whisking constantly.
- Return the mixture to the saucepan and cook over medium heat, stirring continuously until it thickens.
- Remove from heat and let it cool.

5. Assemble Religieuse:

- Cut the cooled choux pastry rounds in half horizontally.
- Fill the bottom half of each round with pastry cream.
- Place the top half back on and press gently to sandwich them together.

6. Make Chocolate Glaze:

- In a heatproof bowl, melt the chopped dark chocolate with the heavy cream over a double boiler or in the microwave. Stir until smooth.
- Add the butter and continue stirring until the glaze is glossy.

7. Glaze the Religieuse:

- Dip the top of each assembled religieuse into the chocolate glaze, ensuring it covers the entire surface.

8. Serve:

- Allow the chocolate glaze to set before serving the religieuse. Enjoy the delightful combination of choux pastry and creamy filling!

A Religieuse is a traditional French pastry that consists of two choux pastry rounds filled with pastry cream, stacked on top of each other, and coated with chocolate glaze. It's a delightful and visually appealing treat.

Gougères

Ingredients:

    1 cup water
    1/2 cup (1 stick) unsalted butter
    1 teaspoon salt
    1 cup all-purpose flour
    4 large eggs
    1 1/2 cups grated Gruyère or Swiss cheese
    1/2 teaspoon black pepper (optional)
    1/4 teaspoon ground nutmeg (optional)
    Egg wash (1 egg beaten with a little water, for brushing)

Instructions:

1. Preheat Oven:

   - Preheat your oven to 375°F (190°C). Line a baking sheet with parchment paper.

2. Prepare Dough:

   - In a medium saucepan, combine water, butter, and salt. Bring to a boil over medium heat.

3. Add Flour:

   - Add the flour all at once and stir vigorously with a wooden spoon until the mixture forms a smooth ball. Continue stirring for about 1-2 minutes to slightly cook the flour.

4. Cool Slightly:

   - Remove the saucepan from heat and let the dough cool for a few minutes.

5. Add Eggs:

   - Add the eggs one at a time, beating well after each addition. The dough should be smooth and glossy.

6. Incorporate Cheese and Seasonings:

- Stir in the grated Gruyère or Swiss cheese. Add black pepper and ground nutmeg if desired, and mix until well combined.

7. Pipe or Spoon:

- Transfer the dough to a piping bag fitted with a large round tip or use two spoons to drop mounds onto the prepared baking sheet. Each mound should be about 1 to 1.5 inches in diameter.

8. Brush with Egg Wash:

- Brush the top of each gougère with the egg wash to create a shiny finish during baking.

9. Bake:

- Bake in the preheated oven for 25-30 minutes or until the gougères are puffed, golden brown, and crispy.

10. Cool:

- Allow the gougères to cool on a wire rack before serving.

11. Serve:

- Serve the gougères as a delightful appetizer or snack. These cheesy and savory pastries are best enjoyed fresh out of the oven.

Gougères are French cheese puffs made with choux pastry and grated cheese. They are a popular and delicious appetizer, perfect for serving at parties or as a savory addition to any meal.

Quiche Lorraine

Ingredients:

For the Pie Crust:

    1 1/4 cups all-purpose flour
    1/2 cup unsalted butter, cold and diced
    1/4 teaspoon salt
    3-4 tablespoons ice water

For the Filling:

5. 8 slices bacon, cooked and crumbled

    1 1/2 cups shredded Gruyère or Swiss cheese
    1 tablespoon all-purpose flour
    1 cup heavy cream
    1/2 cup whole milk
    4 large eggs
    1/4 teaspoon salt
    1/4 teaspoon black pepper
    1/4 teaspoon ground nutmeg (optional)

Instructions:

1. Prepare Pie Crust:

- In a food processor, combine the flour, cold diced butter, and salt. Pulse until the mixture resembles coarse crumbs.
- Add ice water, one tablespoon at a time, pulsing until the dough comes together. Do not overmix.
- Form the dough into a disk, wrap it in plastic wrap, and refrigerate for at least 30 minutes.

2. Preheat Oven:

- Preheat your oven to 375°F (190°C).

3. Roll Out and Line Pie Pan:

- On a floured surface, roll out the chilled dough into a circle large enough to fit a 9-inch pie pan. Transfer the rolled-out dough to the pie pan, pressing it gently into the bottom and up the sides.

4. Blind Bake the Crust:

    - Line the pie crust with parchment paper and fill it with pie weights or dried beans. Bake in the preheated oven for about 15 minutes.
    - Remove the weights and parchment paper, then bake for an additional 5 minutes until the crust is golden. Remove from the oven and et it cool.

5. Prepare Filling:

    - In a bowl, toss the shredded Gruyère or Swiss cheese with 1 tablespoon of flour. Sprinkle the cheese mixture over the cooled pie crust.
    - Scatter the cooked and crumbled bacon over the cheese.

6. Make Quiche Filling:

    - In a separate bowl, whisk together the heavy cream, whole milk, eggs, salt, black pepper, and nutmeg (if using).

7. Pour Filling and Bake:

    - Pour the egg mixture over the cheese and bacon in the pie crust.
    - Bake in the preheated oven for 35-40 minutes or until the quiche is set and golden brown on top.

8. Cool and Serve:

    - Allow the quiche to cool for a few minutes before slicing. Serve warm or at room temperature.

9. Optional: Garnish:

    - Garnish with a sprinkle of additional nutmeg or fresh herbs if desired.

Quiche Lorraine is a classic French savory tart that combines a buttery crust with a rich and creamy filling of bacon, cheese, and a flavorful custard. It makes for a delicious brunch, lunch, or dinner option.

Crêpes

Ingredients:

- 1 cup all-purpose flour
- 2 large eggs
- 1/2 cup whole milk
- 1/2 cup water
- 2 tablespoons unsalted butter, melted
- 1 tablespoon granulated sugar (for sweet crêpes, optional)
- 1/4 teaspoon salt
- Additional butter or oil for greasing the pan

Instructions:

1. Prepare Batter:

- In a blender, combine flour, eggs, milk, water, melted butter, sugar (if making sweet crêpes), and salt. Blend until the batter is smooth. Let the batter rest in the refrigerator for at least 30 minutes, or overnight for best results.

2. Heat the Crêpe Pan:

- Heat a crêpe pan or non-stick skillet over medium heat. Add a small amount of butter or oil and spread it evenly to coat the pan.

3. Pour and Swirl:

- Pour a small amount of batter into the center of the hot pan, lifting it off the heat. Quickly tilt and rotate the pan to spread the batter thinly across the bottom.

4. Cook:

- Cook the crêpe for about 1-2 minutes until the edges start to lift and the bottom is lightly golden. Use a spatula to flip the crêpe and cook for an additional 30 seconds to 1 minute on the other side.

5. Repeat:

- Repeat the process with the remaining batter, adding a little more butter or oil to the pan as needed.

6. Serve:

- Serve the crêpes warm with your favorite toppings. For sweet crêpes, you can use Nutella, whipped cream, fresh fruit, or jam. For savory crêpes, try fillings like ham and cheese, spinach and feta, or sautéed mushrooms.

7. Enjoy:

- Enjoy these versatile and delicious crêpes for breakfast, brunch, or dessert.

Tips:

- Adjust the consistency of the batter by adding more milk or water if needed.
- Experiment with different fillings and toppings to suit your preferences.
- Crêpes can be made ahead of time and stored, separated by sheets of parchment paper, in the refrigerator. Reheat gently before serving.

Crêpes are a classic French treat that can be enjoyed in various ways. Whether you prefer sweet or savory, crêpes offer a versatile and delicious canvas for your favorite fillings and toppings.

Cannele de Bordeaux

Ingredients:

    2 cups whole milk
    1 1/2 tablespoons unsalted butter
    1 vanilla bean, split lengthwise (or 1 teaspoon vanilla extract)
    1 1/4 cups all-purpose flour
    2 cups granulated sugar
    4 large eggs
    1/4 cup dark rum
    Pinch of salt
    Butter and flour for greasing the molds

Instructions:

1. Prepare the Batter:

- In a saucepan, heat the milk and butter over medium heat. If using a vanilla bean, scrape the seeds into the milk and add the bean itself. Bring the mixture to a simmer, then remove from heat and let it cool.

2. Mix Flour and Sugar:

- In a bowl, whisk together the flour and sugar.

3. Add Eggs:

- In a separate bowl, beat the eggs. Gradually add the beaten eggs to the flour and sugar mixture, stirring continuously to avoid lumps.

4. Combine with Milk Mixture:

- Gradually pour the cooled milk mixture into the batter, stirring constantly to create a smooth batter. If using vanilla extract, add it at this stage.

5. Add Rum and Salt:

- Stir in the rum and a pinch of salt. Mix well.

6. Rest the Batter:

    - Cover the batter and let it rest in the refrigerator for at least 24 hours. This resting period is crucial for the development of the cannelé's unique texture and flavor.

7. Preheat Oven and Prepare Molds:

    - Preheat your oven to 450°F (230°C). Butter and flour the cannelé molds thoroughly, ensuring they are well-coated.

8. Fill Molds:

    - Fill each mold with the batter, leaving a little space at the top for the cannelés to rise.

9. Bake:

    - Bake in the preheated oven for 15 minutes, then reduce the heat to 375°F (190°C) and continue baking for another 45-50 minutes or until the cannelés are dark brown and caramelized on the outside.

10. Cool:

    - Allow the cannelés to cool in the molds for a few minutes before transferring them to a wire rack.

11. Serve:

    - Serve the cannelés at room temperature. They are best enjoyed within a day or two of baking.

Tips:

- If you don't have cannelé molds, you can use silicone molds or small, cylindrical molds for similar results.
- Adjust the baking time if using a different-sized mold.

Cannelés de Bordeaux are small French pastries with a caramelized exterior and a soft, custardy interior. The unique shape and rich flavor make them a delightful treat, perfect for enjoying with coffee or as a dessert.

Baba au Rhum

Ingredients:

For the Baba Dough:

> 3 1/2 cups all-purpose flour
> 1/4 cup granulated sugar
> 2 1/4 teaspoons active dry yeast
> 1/2 cup warm milk
> 4 large eggs
> 1/2 cup unsalted butter, softened
> 1/4 teaspoon salt

For the Rum Syrup:

8. 1 cup water

> 1 cup granulated sugar
> 1 cup dark rum

For Garnish:

11. Whipped cream

> Fresh fruit (such as berries or sliced citrus)

Instructions:

1. Prepare Baba Dough:

- In a small bowl, combine warm milk and active dry yeast. Let it sit for 5-10 minutes until frothy.
- In a large bowl, combine flour, sugar, and salt. Make a well in the center and add the yeast mixture, eggs, and softened butter.
- Mix the ingredients to form a dough. Knead the dough on a floured surface until smooth and elastic.

- Place the dough back in the bowl, cover it with a kitchen towel, and let it rise in a warm place for about 1-2 hours, or until it has doubled in size.

2. Shape and Bake Babas:

- Preheat your oven to 375°F (190°C).
- Grease baba molds or muffin tins. Divide the dough into portions and shape them into rounds. Place each round into a mold.
- Bake in the preheated oven for 15-20 minutes or until the babas are golden brown and sound hollow when tapped. Allow them to cool.

3. Prepare Rum Syrup:

- In a saucepan, combine water and sugar. Bring to a boil, stirring until the sugar dissolves.
- Remove from heat and let the syrup cool to room temperature.
- Stir in the dark rum.

4. Soak the Babas:

- Once the babas have cooled, place them in a shallow dish. Pour the rum syrup over the babas, ensuring they are well-soaked. Let them absorb the syrup for at least 1-2 hours, or overnight.

5. Garnish and Serve:

- Before serving, top the babas with whipped cream and fresh fruit.
- Serve the Baba au Rhum as a delightful, boozy dessert.

Tips:

- You can customize the level of rum flavor by adjusting the amount of syrup soaked into the babas.
- Feel free to experiment with different fruits and toppings for added variety.

Baba au Rhum is a classic French dessert known for its rich, rum-soaked cake. It's a delightful treat that brings together the sweetness of the cake, the warmth of rum, and the freshness of whipped cream and fruit.

Clafoutis

Ingredients:

    1 1/2 cups whole milk
    3/4 cup granulated sugar
    3 large eggs
    1 tablespoon vanilla extract
    1 cup all-purpose flour
    1/4 teaspoon salt
    Butter for greasing the baking dish
    2 cups fresh cherries, pitted (traditional) or other fruits like berries, sliced peaches, or plums
    Powdered sugar for dusting (optional)

Instructions:

1. Preheat Oven:

   - Preheat your oven to 350°F (175°C). Grease a baking dish (typically a round 9-inch dish) with butter.

2. Prepare the Batter:

   - In a blender, combine milk, sugar, eggs, vanilla extract, flour, and salt. Blend until the batter is smooth and well combined.

3. Rest the Batter:

   - Allow the batter to rest for about 15-20 minutes. This helps the flour to fully absorb the liquid.

4. Arrange Fruits:

   - Arrange the pitted cherries or other fruits in the greased baking dish.

5. Pour Batter:

   - Pour the rested batter over the fruits in the baking dish.

6. Bake:

   - Bake in the preheated oven for approximately 45-50 minutes or until the clafoutis is set in the center and the top is golden brown.

7. Cool:

   - Allow the clafoutis to cool for a few minutes before slicing. It can be served warm or at room temperature.

8. Dust with Powdered Sugar:

   - Optionally, dust the clafoutis with powdered sugar before serving.

9. Serve:

   - Serve slices of clafoutis on plates, either on its own or with a dollop of whipped cream or a scoop of vanilla ice cream.

Tips:

   - Traditional clafoutis uses cherries with pits, as they are believed to enhance the flavor. However, you can pit the cherries if you prefer.
   - Experiment with different fruits based on the season for variety.
   - Clafoutis is often served for breakfast or dessert.

Clafoutis is a delightful French dessert that's easy to make and showcases the sweetness of seasonal fruits. It has a custard-like texture and is a perfect way to enjoy the bounty of fresh fruits when they're in season.

Tarte au Citron (Lemon Tart)

Ingredients:

For the Tart Crust:

    1 1/4 cups all-purpose flour
    1/2 cup unsalted butter, cold and diced
    1/4 cup granulated sugar
    1 large egg yolk
    1-2 tablespoons ice water

For the Lemon Filling:

6. 4-5 large lemons (for zest and juice)

    1 cup granulated sugar
    4 large eggs
    1/2 cup unsalted butter, melted

For Garnish:

10. Powdered sugar

    Fresh berries or mint leaves (optional)

Instructions:

1. Prepare Tart Crust:

- In a food processor, combine flour, cold diced butter, and sugar. Pulse until the mixture resembles coarse crumbs.
- Add the egg yolk and pulse again. Gradually add ice water, one tablespoon at a time, until the dough comes together.
- Form the dough into a disk, wrap it in plastic wrap, and refrigerate for at least 30 minutes.

2. Roll Out and Line Tart Pan:

   - Preheat your oven to 375°F (190°C).
   - On a floured surface, roll out the chilled dough into a circle large enough to fit a 9-inch tart pan. Transfer the rolled-out dough to the tart pan, pressing it gently into the bottom and up the sides. Trim any excess dough.

3. Blind Bake the Crust:

   - Line the tart crust with parchment paper and fill it with pie weights or dried beans. Bake in the preheated oven for about 15 minutes.
   - Remove the weights and parchment paper, then bake for an additional 5 minutes until the crust is golden. Allow it to cool.

4. Prepare Lemon Filling:

   - Zest and juice the lemons. You should have about 1/2 cup of lemon juice.
   - In a bowl, whisk together sugar and eggs until well combined.
   - Gradually whisk in the melted butter, followed by the lemon zest and juice. Mix until smooth.

5. Bake the Lemon Tart:

   - Pour the lemon filling into the pre-baked tart crust.
   - Bake in the preheated oven for 20-25 minutes or until the filling is set and has a slight jiggle in the center.

6. Cool and Garnish:

   - Allow the lemon tart to cool in the tart pan on a wire rack. Once cooled, refrigerate for at least 2 hours to chill.
   - Before serving, dust the tart with powdered sugar and garnish with fresh berries or mint leaves if desired.

7. Serve:

   - Slice and serve the Tarte au Citron for a refreshing and tangy dessert.

Tips:

- Adjust the sweetness and tartness of the filling according to your preference by tweaking the amount of sugar and lemon juice.
- You can make the tart crust in advance and freeze it for later use.

Tarte au Citron is a classic French dessert that beautifully balances the sweetness of the lemon filling with a buttery tart crust. It's a perfect treat for citrus lovers and a delightful way to end a meal.

Pain Perdu (French Toast)

Ingredients:

    4 slices of day-old bread (such as French bread or brioche)
    2 large eggs
    1/2 cup milk
    1 tablespoon granulated sugar
    1/2 teaspoon vanilla extract
    1/4 teaspoon ground cinnamon (optional)
    Pinch of salt
    Butter or oil for cooking
    Maple syrup, powdered sugar, or fresh fruit for serving

Instructions:

1. Prepare the Bread:

- If the bread is not already sliced, cut it into thick slices. Day-old bread works best as it absorbs the egg mixture without becoming too soggy.

2. Make the Egg Mixture:

- In a shallow dish, whisk together eggs, milk, sugar, vanilla extract, ground cinnamon (if using), and a pinch of salt. Ensure that the mixture is well-combined.

3. Soak the Bread:

- Dip each slice of bread into the egg mixture, ensuring both sides are coated. Allow the bread to soak for about 20-30 seconds per side, depending on the thickness of the bread.

4. Heat the Pan:

- Heat a skillet or griddle over medium heat. Add a small amount of butter or oil to coat the surface.

5. Cook the French Toast:

- Place the soaked bread slices on the hot skillet. Cook for 2-3 minutes on each side or until golden brown and cooked through.

6. Keep Warm:

- Keep the cooked French toast warm in a low oven while you cook the remaining slices.

7. Serve:

- Serve the Pain Perdu hot with your choice of toppings. Drizzle with maple syrup, dust with powdered sugar, or add fresh fruit for a delightful touch.

8. Enjoy:

- Enjoy the deliciously indulgent and comforting Pain Perdu as a delightful breakfast or brunch treat.

Tips:

- Experiment with different bread varieties like challah, baguette, or cinnamon swirl bread for varied flavors.
- Customize your toppings with whipped cream, yogurt, or a sprinkle of your favorite nuts.
- For extra richness, you can add a dash of cream to the egg mixture.

Pain Perdu, or French Toast, is a classic breakfast dish that turns day-old bread into a delicious and satisfying meal. With its simple preparation and endless topping possibilities, it's a versatile and beloved dish enjoyed by many.

Tarte Normande

Ingredients:

For the Tart Crust:

    1 1/4 cups all-purpose flour
    1/2 cup unsalted butter, cold and diced
    1/4 cup granulated sugar
    1 large egg yolk
    1-2 tablespoons ice water

For the Apple Filling:

6. 4-5 large apples (such as Granny Smith or Braeburn), peeled, cored, and sliced

    2 tablespoons unsalted butter
    1/4 cup granulated sugar
    1 teaspoon ground cinnamon

For the Custard:

10. 2 large eggs

    1/2 cup granulated sugar
    1/2 cup heavy cream
    1/4 cup whole milk
    1 teaspoon vanilla extract

Instructions:

1. Prepare Tart Crust:

- In a food processor, combine flour, cold diced butter, and sugar. Pulse until the mixture resembles coarse crumbs.
- Add the egg yolk and pulse again. Gradually add ice water, one tablespoon at a time, until the dough comes together.

- Form the dough into a disk, wrap it in plastic wrap, and refrigerate for at least 30 minutes.

2. Roll Out and Line Tart Pan:

    - Preheat your oven to 375°F (190°C).
    - On a floured surface, roll out the chilled dough into a circle large enough to fit a 9-inch tart pan. Transfer the rolled-out dough to the tart pan, pressing it gently into the bottom and up the sides. Trim any excess dough.

3. Prepare Apple Filling:

    - In a skillet, melt the butter over medium heat. Add the sliced apples, sugar, and ground cinnamon. Cook for about 5-7 minutes or until the apples are softened. Remove from heat and let them cool slightly.

4. Arrange Apples in Tart Crust:

    - Arrange the cooked apple slices evenly over the prepared tart crust.

5. Prepare Custard:

    - In a bowl, whisk together eggs, sugar, heavy cream, whole milk, and vanilla extract until well combined.

6. Pour Custard Over Apples:

    - Pour the custard mixture over the arranged apples in the tart crust.

7. Bake:

    - Bake in the preheated oven for approximately 35-40 minutes or until the custard is set and the top is golden brown.

8. Cool and Serve:

- Allow the Tarte Normande to cool in the tart pan on a wire rack. Once cooled, remove it from the pan.
- Serve slices of the tart at room temperature.

9. Optional: Glaze:

- Optionally, you can brush the top of the cooled tart with a light apricot glaze for a shiny finish.

10. Enjoy:

- Enjoy the delicious Tarte Normande with its rich custard, tender apples, and buttery crust.

Tips:

- You can use a variety of apples for a more complex flavor.
- Experiment with adding a sprinkle of chopped nuts, such as almonds or walnuts for added texture.

Tarte Normande is a delightful French dessert that combines the sweetness of apples with a rich custard, all encased in a buttery tart crust. It's a wonderful treat that captures the flavors of Normandy.

Saint-Honoré Cake

Ingredients:

For the Puff Pastry Base:

    1 sheet of puff pastry, thawed if frozen
    1 tablespoon granulated sugar (for sprinkling)

For the Choux Pastry (Pâte à Choux):

3. 1/2 cup water

    1/2 cup whole milk
    1/2 cup (1 stick) unsalted butter
    1 tablespoon granulated sugar
    1/4 teaspoon salt
    1 cup all-purpose flour
    4 large eggs

For the Diplomat Cream:

10. 2 cups whole milk

    1/2 cup granulated sugar
    4 large egg yolks
    1/4 cup cornstarch
    1 teaspoon vanilla extract
    1 cup heavy cream, whipped to stiff peaks

For the Caramel:

16. 1 cup granulated sugar

    1/4 cup water

For Assembly:

18. Whipped cream for decoration

Choux pastry filled with whipped cream

Instructions:

1. Preheat Oven:

- Preheat your oven to 400°F (200°C).

2. Prepare Puff Pastry Base:

- Roll out the puff pastry sheet and cut it into a round shape. Place it on a parchment-lined baking sheet. Sprinkle the surface with granulated sugar.
- Bake in the preheated oven for about 15-20 minutes or until the puff pastry is golden and puffed. Allow it to cool.

3. Make Choux Pastry:

- In a saucepan, combine water, milk, butter, sugar, and salt. Bring to a boil.
- Add the flour all at once and stir vigorously until the mixture forms a smooth ball.
- Transfer the dough to a mixing bowl and let it cool for a few minutes.
- Add the eggs one at a time, beating well after each addition, until the dough is smooth and glossy.
- Transfer the choux pastry to a piping bag fitted with a round tip.

4. Pipe Choux Puffs:

- Pipe small rounds of choux pastry around the edge of the baked puff pastry base.

5. Bake Choux Puffs:

- Bake in the preheated oven for 20-25 minutes or until the choux puffs are golden brown and crisp. Let them cool.

6. Prepare Diplomat Cream:

- In a saucepan, heat milk until hot but not boiling. In a bowl, whisk together egg yolks, sugar, cornstarch, and vanilla extract.
- Slowly pour the hot milk into the egg mixture, whisking constantly.

- Return the mixture to the saucepan and cook over medium heat, stirring continuously until it thickens.
- Allow the pastry cream to cool completely.
- Once cooled, fold in the whipped cream to create the diplomat cream.

7. Assemble Saint-Honoré Cake:

- Fill the choux puffs with diplomat cream using a piping bag.
- In a separate saucepan, make caramel by heating sugar and water until it turns amber in color.
- Dip the filled choux puffs into the caramel and arrange them on top of the puff pastry base.
- Optionally, pipe additional whipped cream on top of the choux puffs for decoration.

8. Serve:

- Slice and serve the Saint-Honoré Cake, enjoying the combination of crispy puff pastry, creamy diplomat cream, and caramelized choux puffs.

Tips:

- Be cautious when working with hot caramel to avoid burns.
- You can customize the size of the Saint-Honoré Cake by adjusting the dimensions of the puff pastry base and the number of choux puffs.
- Serve the cake on the day of assembly for the best texture and flavor.

Pissaladière

Ingredients:

For the Dough:

    2 1/4 cups all-purpose flour
    1 teaspoon active dry yeast
    1 teaspoon sugar
    1/2 teaspoon salt
    1 cup warm water
    2 tablespoons olive oil

For the Topping:

7. 2 tablespoons olive oil

    4 large yellow onions, thinly sliced
    2 cloves garlic, minced
    1 tablespoon fresh thyme leaves
    1/2 teaspoon salt
    1/4 teaspoon black pepper
    1/2 cup black olives, pitted and halved (Nicoise olives are traditional)
    6-8 anchovy fillets, drained and halved lengthwise
    Optional: 1 tablespoon capers

Instructions:

1. Prepare the Dough:

- In a small bowl, combine warm water, sugar, and yeast. Let it sit for about 5-10 minutes until frothy.
- In a large mixing bowl, combine flour and salt. Make a well in the center and pour in the activated yeast mixture and olive oil.
- Mix until a dough forms. Knead the dough on a floured surface until smooth and elastic. Place the dough in a lightly oiled bowl, cover with a kitchen towel, and let it rise in a warm place for about 1-2 hours or until doubled in size.

2. Prepare the Topping:

- While the dough is rising, heat olive oil in a large skillet over medium-low heat. Add sliced onions, garlic, thyme, salt, and black pepper. Cook, stirring occasionally, until the onions are soft and caramelized (about 20-30 minutes).
- Let the onion mixture cool to room temperature.

3. Preheat Oven:

- Preheat your oven to 425°F (220°C).

4. Roll Out the Dough:

- Roll out the risen dough on a floured surface to fit a baking sheet or pizza stone.

5. Assemble the Pissaladière:

- Transfer the rolled-out dough to the baking sheet or pizza stone.
- Spread the caramelized onion mixture evenly over the dough, leaving a border around the edges.
- Arrange the halved black olives, anchovy fillets, and capers (if using) over the onions.

6. Bake:

- Bake in the preheated oven for 20-25 minutes or until the crust is golden brown and the toppings are slightly crispy.

7. Serve:

- Let the Pissaladière cool for a few minutes before slicing. Serve warm or at room temperature.

8. Enjoy:

- Enjoy this classic Provençal dish as an appetizer, snack, or light meal.

Tips:

- You can customize the topping with additional herbs like rosemary or oregano.
- Pissaladière can be enjoyed warm or at room temperature and is a great addition to picnics or gatherings.

Flan Parisien

Ingredients:

For the Pastry:

    1 1/4 cups all-purpose flour
    1/2 cup unsalted butter, cold and diced
    1/4 cup granulated sugar
    1 large egg

For the Custard Filling:

5. 2 cups whole milk

    1 cup heavy cream
    1 vanilla bean, split lengthwise (or 1 teaspoon vanilla extract)
    6 large egg yolks
    1 cup granulated sugar
    1/2 cup cornstarch

For Caramel Glaze:

11. 1/2 cup granulated sugar

    2 tablespoons water

Instructions:

1. Prepare the Pastry:

- In a food processor, combine flour, cold diced butter, and sugar. Pulse until the mixture resembles coarse crumbs.
- Add the egg and pulse again until the dough comes together. Form the dough into a disk, wrap it in plastic wrap, and refrigerate for at least 30 minutes.

2. Roll Out the Pastry:

- Preheat your oven to 375°F (190°C).
- On a floured surface, roll out the chilled dough into a circle large enough to fit a 9-inch tart pan. Transfer the rolled-out dough to the tart pan, pressing it gently into the bottom and up the sides. Trim any excess dough.

3. Prepare the Custard Filling:

- In a saucepan, combine whole milk, heavy cream, and the split vanilla bean. Bring the mixture to a simmer over medium heat, then remove from heat and let it cool. If using vanilla extract, add it after removing from heat.
- In a bowl, whisk together egg yolks, sugar, and cornstarch until well combined.
- Gradually pour the cooled milk mixture over the egg yolk mixture, whisking constantly.
- Strain the custard mixture to remove the vanilla bean or any curdled bits.

4. Bake the Flan:

- Pour the custard into the prepared tart shell.
- Bake in the preheated oven for 35-40 minutes or until the custard is set and the top is golden brown.

5. Prepare Caramel Glaze:

- In a saucepan, combine sugar and water over medium heat. Cook, without stirring, until the sugar caramelizes and turns a golden brown color.
- Pour the caramel over the baked flan, spreading it evenly.

6. Cool and Serve:

- Allow the Flan Parisien to cool completely in the tart pan on a wire rack.
- Once cooled, remove from the tart pan, slice, and serve.

7. Enjoy:

- Enjoy the creamy and caramelized goodness of Flan Parisien as a delightful dessert.

Tips:

- You can use vanilla extract instead of a vanilla bean for convenience.
- Be cautious when working with hot caramel, as it can cause burns. Exercise care and attention during this step.

Tarte à l'Oignon (Onion Tart)

Ingredients:

For the Pastry:

    1 1/4 cups all-purpose flour
    1/2 cup unsalted butter, cold and diced
    1/4 teaspoon salt
    3-4 tablespoons ice water

For the Onion Filling:

5. 3 large onions, thinly sliced

    2 tablespoons unsalted butter
    1 tablespoon olive oil
    2 teaspoons fresh thyme leaves (or 1 teaspoon dried thyme)
    Salt and black pepper, to taste
    2 large eggs
    1/2 cup heavy cream
    1/2 cup milk
    1/2 cup grated Gruyère or Swiss cheese (optional)

Instructions:

1. Prepare the Pastry:

- In a food processor, combine flour, cold diced butter, and salt. Pulse until the mixture resembles coarse crumbs.
- Add ice water, one tablespoon at a time, pulsing until the dough comes together. Do not overmix.
- Form the dough into a disk, wrap it in plastic wrap, and refrigerate for at least 30 minutes.

2. Roll Out and Line Tart Pan:

- Preheat your oven to 375°F (190°C).

- On a floured surface, roll out the chilled dough into a circle large enough to fit a 9-inch tart pan. Transfer the rolled-out dough to the tart pan, pressing it gently into the bottom and up the sides. Trim any excess dough.

3. Prepare the Onion Filling:

    - In a large skillet, heat butter and olive oil over medium-low heat. Add the thinly sliced onions and cook, stirring occasionally, until the onions are soft and golden brown (about 20-30 minutes).
    - Stir in fresh thyme, salt, and black pepper. Remove from heat and let it cool slightly.

4. Assemble the Tart:

    - Spread the caramelized onion mixture evenly over the prepared tart crust.

5. Prepare the Custard Filling:

    - In a bowl, whisk together eggs, heavy cream, and milk until well combined.

6. Pour Custard Over Onions:

    - Pour the custard mixture over the caramelized onions in the tart crust.

7. Optional: Add Cheese:

    - If desired, sprinkle grated Gruyère or Swiss cheese over the top.

8. Bake:

    - Bake in the preheated oven for 30-35 minutes or until the custard is set and the top is golden brown.

9. Cool and Serve:

    - Allow the Tarte à l'Oignon to cool for a few minutes before slicing. Serve warm or at room temperature.

10. Enjoy:

- Enjoy the savory and flavorful Onion Tart as a delightful appetizer or light meal.

Tips:

- Customize the tart by adding cooked bacon or sautéed mushrooms to the onion filling.
- Serve the tart with a side salad for a complete meal.

Far Breton

Ingredients:

    2 cups whole milk
    1 cup all-purpose flour
    1/2 cup granulated sugar
    4 large eggs
    1/4 teaspoon salt
    1 teaspoon vanilla extract
    1/2 cup prunes, pitted and chopped
    Butter for greasing the baking dish

Instructions:

1. Prepare the Prunes:

- If the prunes are not pitted, pit and chop them into smaller pieces.

2. Preheat Oven:

- Preheat your oven to 350°F (175°C). Grease a baking dish (usually a round dish of about 9-10 inches in diameter) with butter.

3. Make the Batter:

- In a blender or mixing bowl, combine milk, flour, sugar, eggs, salt, and vanilla extract. Blend or whisk until you have a smooth batter.

4. Arrange Prunes:

- Place the chopped prunes evenly in the greased baking dish.

5. Pour Batter Over Prunes:

- Pour the batter over the prunes in the baking dish.

6. Bake:

- Bake in the preheated oven for approximately 45-50 minutes or until the Far is set and has a golden brown color on top.

7. Cool:

- Allow the Far Breton to cool in the baking dish for a bit before slicing.

8. Serve:

- Slice the Far Breton into wedges and serve either warm or at room temperature.

9. Enjoy:

- Enjoy this classic Breton dessert with a cup of tea or coffee.

Tips:

- Some variations of Far Breton include adding a splash of rum or dark rum-soaked prunes for extra flavor.
- You can experiment with different dried fruits or even add a hint of orange zest to the batter for a citrusy twist.

Far Breton is a traditional Breton dessert that is a cross between a custard and a cake. It's a simple yet delightful treat, perfect for enjoying the rich flavors of prunes in a comforting, baked dish.

Pain d'Épices (French Spice Bread)

Ingredients:

    1 cup all-purpose flour
    1/2 cup rye flour
    1 teaspoon baking powder
    1/2 teaspoon baking soda
    1 teaspoon ground cinnamon
    1/2 teaspoon ground ginger
    1/4 teaspoon ground nutmeg
    1/4 teaspoon ground cloves
    1/4 teaspoon salt
    1/2 cup unsalted butter, softened
    1/2 cup honey
    1/2 cup dark molasses
    1/2 cup brown sugar, packed
    2 large eggs
    1 cup buttermilk

Instructions:

1. Preheat Oven:

- Preheat your oven to 325°F (165°C). Grease and flour a loaf pan.

2. Combine Dry Ingredients:

- In a medium bowl, whisk together all-purpose flour, rye flour, baking powder, baking soda, ground cinnamon, ground ginger, ground nutmeg, ground cloves, and salt. Set aside.

3. Cream Butter and Sugar:

- In a large bowl, cream together the softened butter and brown sugar until light and fluffy.

4. Add Honey, Molasses, and Eggs:

- Add the honey and molasses to the butter-sugar mixture. Mix well. Add the eggs one at a time, beating well after each addition.

5. Alternate Adding Dry Ingredients and Buttermilk:

- Gradually add the dry ingredients to the wet ingredients, alternating with buttermilk. Begin and end with the dry ingredients. Mix until just combined.

6. Pour Batter into Pan:

- Pour the batter into the prepared loaf pan, spreading it evenly.

7. Bake:

- Bake in the preheated oven for approximately 50-60 minutes or until a toothpick inserted into the center comes out clean.

8. Cool:

- Allow the Pain d'Épices to cool in the pan for about 10 minutes, then transfer it to a wire rack to cool completely.

9. Slice and Serve:

- Once cooled, slice the spice bread and serve. It can be enjoyed on its own or with butter.

10. Optional: Age the Bread:

- For a more traditional approach, you can wrap the cooled Pain d'Épices in parchment paper and let it age for a day or two before slicing. This allows the flavors to deepen.

11. Enjoy:

- Enjoy the rich and aromatic flavors of this French Spice Bread!

Tips:

- Adjust the spice levels to your preference by tweaking the amounts of cinnamon, ginger, nutmeg, and cloves.
- Feel free to add chopped nuts or dried fruits for added texture and flavor.
- This bread tends to improve in flavor over time, so consider making it a day ahead for a richer taste.

Mousse au Chocolat

Ingredients:

    7 ounces (200g) high-quality dark chocolate, finely chopped
    3 large eggs, separated
    1/4 cup (50g) granulated sugar
    1 cup (240ml) heavy cream
    1 teaspoon pure vanilla extract (optional)
    A pinch of salt

Instructions:

1. Melt the Chocolate:

- In a heatproof bowl, melt the chopped chocolate over a double boiler or in the microwave in short intervals, stirring until smooth. Let it cool slightly.

2. Separate the Eggs:

- Separate the egg yolks from the whites, placing each in a different bowl. Ensure that there is no trace of yolk in the whites.

3. Beat the Egg Yolks:

- Beat the egg yolks with half of the sugar until the mixture is pale and slightly thickened.

4. Incorporate Chocolate:

- Gradually add the melted chocolate to the egg yolk mixture, stirring well to combine. If using vanilla extract, add it at this stage.

5. Whip the Egg Whites:

- In a clean, dry bowl, whip the egg whites with a pinch of salt until soft peaks form. Gradually add the remaining sugar and continue to whip until glossy and stiff peaks form.

6. Whip the Cream:

- In another bowl, whip the heavy cream until stiff peaks form.

7. Combine:

    - Gently fold the whipped egg whites into the chocolate mixture until well combined. Be gentle to maintain the mousse's light and airy texture.

8. Fold in the Whipped Cream:

    - Next, fold in the whipped cream until the mousse is smooth and evenly combined.

9. Chill:

    - Spoon the chocolate mousse into serving glasses or bowls. Refrigerate for at least 2-3 hours or until set.

10. Garnish and Serve:

    - Before serving, garnish the chocolate mousse with grated chocolate, whipped cream, or berries if desired.

11. Enjoy:

    - Serve and enjoy the luxurious and velvety texture of homemade Mousse au Chocolat.

Tips:

- Use high-quality chocolate for the best flavor. Dark chocolate with a cocoa content of around 70% works well.
- Ensure that the melted chocolate has cooled slightly before incorporating it into the egg yolk mixture to prevent the eggs from scrambling.
- For a variety of flavors, you can add a splash of liqueur, such as Grand Marnier or coffee liqueur, to the chocolate mixture.

Tartelette aux Framboises (Raspberry Tartlet)

Ingredients:

For the Tart Crust:

    1 1/4 cups all-purpose flour
    1/2 cup unsalted butter, cold and diced
    1/4 cup granulated sugar
    1 large egg yolk
    1-2 tablespoons ice water

For the Pastry Cream:

6. 1 cup whole milk

    1/2 cup granulated sugar
    3 large egg yolks
    2 tablespoons cornstarch
    1 teaspoon vanilla extract

For Assembly:

11. Fresh raspberries

    Apricot or raspberry jam for glaze
    Powdered sugar for dusting (optional)

Instructions:

1. Prepare the Tart Crust:

- In a food processor, combine flour, cold diced butter, and sugar. Pulse until the mixture resembles coarse crumbs.
- Add the egg yolk and pulse again. Gradually add ice water, one tablespoon at a time, until the dough comes together.
- Form the dough into a disk, wrap it in plastic wrap, and refrigerate for at least 30 minutes.

2. Roll Out and Line Tartlet Pans:

- Preheat your oven to 375°F (190°C).
- On a floured surface, roll out the chilled dough. Cut out circles to fit tartlet pans. Press the dough into the pans, trimming any excess. Prick the bottoms with a fork.

3. Bake the Tartlet Shells:

- Place parchment paper over the tartlet shells and fill them with pie weights or dried beans. Bake in the preheated oven for about 15 minutes. Remove the weights and parchment paper and bake for an additional 5 minutes or until the crusts are golden. Allow them to cool.

4. Prepare the Pastry Cream:

- In a saucepan, heat the milk until it's just about to boil.
- In a bowl, whisk together sugar, egg yolks, and cornstarch until well combined.
- Gradually pour the hot milk into the egg mixture while whisking constantly. Return the mixture to the saucepan.
- Cook over medium heat, stirring constantly, until the mixture thickens.
- Remove from heat, stir in vanilla extract, and let it cool.

5. Assemble the Tartlets:

- Spread a thin layer of pastry cream over the baked tartlet shells.
- Arrange fresh raspberries on top of the pastry cream.

6. Glaze and Garnish:

- Warm the apricot or raspberry jam in a saucepan until it becomes liquid. Brush the berries with the jam to glaze.
- Optionally, dust the tartlets with powdered sugar for a decorative touch.

7. Chill and Serve:

- Refrigerate the tartlets for at least 1-2 hours before serving to set the pastry cream.

8. Enjoy:

- Serve these delightful Tartelettes aux Framboises chilled and savor the combination of buttery crust, creamy pastry cream, and fresh raspberries.

Tips:

- Feel free to experiment with different fruits or a combination of berries for variety.
- Ensure the tartlet shells are fully cooled before adding the pastry cream and berries.
- Use high-quality raspberry or apricot jam for a flavorful glaze.

Gâteau Basque

Ingredients:

For the Dough:

- 2 cups all-purpose flour
- 1 cup unsalted butter, softened
- 1 cup granulated sugar
- 3 large egg yolks
- 1 teaspoon vanilla extract
- 1/2 teaspoon baking powder
- A pinch of salt

For the Pastry Cream (Crème Pâtissière):

8. 2 cups whole milk

- 1 vanilla bean, split (or 1 teaspoon vanilla extract)
- 4 large egg yolks
- 1/2 cup granulated sugar
- 1/3 cup cornstarch

For the Assembly:

13. 1/2 cup fruit preserves (traditionally black cherry or cherry)

- 1 egg yolk (for egg wash)

Instructions:

1. Prepare the Dough:

- In a bowl, cream together the softened butter and sugar until light and fluffy.
- Add the egg yolks one at a time, beating well after each addition. Add the vanilla extract and mix.
- In a separate bowl, whisk together the flour, baking powder, and salt.
- Gradually add the dry ingredients to the wet ingredients, mixing until a soft dough forms. Divide the dough in half, shape each half into a disk, wrap in plastic wrap, and refrigerate for at least 1 hour.

2. Make the Pastry Cream:

    - In a saucepan, heat the milk with the split vanilla bean over medium heat until it is about to boil. Remove from heat and let it infuse for 10-15 minutes. If using vanilla extract, add it after removing from heat.
    - In a bowl, whisk together the egg yolks, sugar, and cornstarch until well combined.
    - Gradually pour the warm milk (strained to remove the vanilla bean) into the egg mixture, whisking constantly.
    - Return the mixture to the saucepan and cook over medium heat, stirring constantly, until it thickens into a pastry cream. Remove from heat and let it cool.

3. Roll Out the Dough:

    - Preheat your oven to 375°F (190°C). Take one of the chilled dough disks and roll it out to fit the bottom of a tart pan or springform pan.

4. Assemble the Gâteau Basque:

    - Place the rolled-out dough in the bottom of the pan. Spread a layer of fruit preserves over the dough, leaving a border around the edges.
    - Spoon the pastry cream over the fruit preserves, spreading it evenly.

5. Add the Top Layer:

    - Roll out the second dough disk and place it over the pastry cream, sealing the edges with the bottom layer.

6. Egg Wash:

    - In a small bowl, beat the egg yolk and brush it over the top of the Gâteau Basque for a golden finish.

7. Bake:

    - Bake in the preheated oven for 30-35 minutes or until the top is golden brown.

8. Cool and Serve:

- Allow the Gâteau Basque to cool in the pan before transferring it to a serving platter. Slice and serve at room temperature.

9. Enjoy:

- Enjoy the rich and flavorful Gâteau Basque, a traditional Basque dessert!

Tips:

- Experiment with different fruit preserves for variety, but traditional choices include black cherry or cherry.
- You can decorate the top with a lattice pattern using the second dough disk or simply leave it plain for a classic look.

Puits d'Amour

Ingredients:

For the Puff Pastry:

    1 sheet of puff pastry (store-bought or homemade)
    1 tablespoon granulated sugar (for sprinkling)

For the Choux Pastry:

3. 1/2 cup water

    4 tablespoons unsalted butter
    1/2 cup all-purpose flour
    2 large eggs
    1 teaspoon vanilla extract

For the Diplomat Cream:

8. 1 cup whole milk

    3 large egg yolks
    1/3 cup granulated sugar
    2 tablespoons cornstarch
    1 teaspoon vanilla extract
    1 cup heavy cream, whipped to stiff peaks

For the Caramel Glaze:

14. 1/2 cup granulated sugar

    1 tablespoon water

Instructions:

1. Prepare the Puff Pastry:

- Preheat your oven to the temperature indicated on the puff pastry package.
- Roll out the puff pastry sheet and cut it into rounds using a round cutter. Place the rounds on a baking sheet lined with parchment paper.
- Sprinkle each round with a little granulated sugar. Bake according to the package instructions or until golden brown and puffed. Allow them to cool.

2. Make the Choux Pastry:

- In a saucepan, bring water and butter to a boil. Add the flour all at once and stir vigorously until the mixture forms a ball. Remove from heat.
- Let the mixture cool for a couple of minutes, then add the eggs one at a time, beating well after each addition. Stir in the vanilla extract.
- Transfer the choux pastry dough to a piping bag fitted with a plain round tip.

3. Pipe Choux Rings:

- Pipe rings of choux pastry onto a baking sheet lined with parchment paper. You can pipe a smaller circle on top of a larger one to form a ring shape.

4. Bake Choux Pastry:

- Bake in the preheated oven (temperature may vary, follow choux pastry recipe instructions) until the choux pastry is golden brown and crisp. Allow them to cool.

5. Prepare Diplomat Cream:

- In a saucepan, heat the milk until it's just about to boil. In a bowl, whisk together egg yolks, sugar, and cornstarch until well combined.
- Gradually pour the hot milk into the egg mixture, whisking constantly. Return the mixture to the saucepan and cook over medium heat, stirring constantly, until it thickens into a pastry cream. Remove from heat, stir in vanilla extract, and let it cool.
- Once the pastry cream is cooled, fold in the whipped cream gently to create a light and airy diplomat cream.

6. Fill the Choux Pastry:

- Cut the cooled choux pastry rings in half horizontally. Pipe or spoon the diplomat cream onto the bottom half of each ring.

7. Make the Caramel Glaze:

- In a small saucepan, combine sugar and water. Cook over medium heat, swirling the pan occasionally, until the sugar caramelizes and turns a golden brown color. Be cautious not to burn it.

8. Glaze the Puits d'Amour:

- Drizzle the caramel glaze over the filled choux pastry rings.

9. Assemble:

- Place the top halves of the choux pastry rings over the diplomat cream and caramel glaze.

10. Enjoy:

- Your Puits d'Amour is now ready to be enjoyed! The combination of crisp choux pastry, delicate diplomat cream, and caramel glaze makes for a delightful treat.

Tips:

- Be careful when working with hot caramel. Use caution to avoid burns.
- You can customize the diplomat cream by adding a hint of citrus zest or a splash of liqueur for extra flavor.

Choux à la Crème

Ingredients:

For the Choux Pastry:

    1 cup water
    1/2 cup unsalted butter
    1 cup all-purpose flour
    4 large eggs
    1/4 teaspoon salt

For the Pastry Cream:

6. 2 cups whole milk

    1/2 cup granulated sugar
    4 large egg yolks
    1/4 cup cornstarch
    1 teaspoon vanilla extract

For Assembly and Decoration:

11. Powdered sugar for dusting

    Chocolate ganache or icing (optional)

Instructions:

1. Prepare the Choux Pastry:

- Preheat your oven to 425°F (220°C). Line baking sheets with parchment paper.
- In a saucepan, combine water, butter, and salt. Bring to a boil over medium heat.
- Add the flour all at once, stirring vigorously until the mixture forms a ball and pulls away from the sides of the pan. Remove from heat and let it cool for a couple of minutes.
- Add the eggs one at a time, beating well after each addition until the batter is smooth.

2. Pipe and Bake:

- Transfer the choux pastry dough to a piping bag fitted with a plain round tip. Pipe small mounds onto the prepared baking sheets, leaving space between each.
- Bake in the preheated oven for 15 minutes, then reduce the temperature to 375°F (190°C) and bake for an additional 20-25 minutes or until the choux are golden brown and sound hollow when tapped.
- Remove from the oven and let them cool on a wire rack.

3. Prepare the Pastry Cream:

- In a saucepan, heat the milk until it's just about to boil.
- In a bowl, whisk together sugar, egg yolks, and cornstarch until well combined.
- Gradually pour the hot milk into the egg mixture while whisking constantly.
- Return the mixture to the saucepan and cook over medium heat, stirring constantly, until the mixture thickens.
- Remove from heat, stir in vanilla extract, and let it cool. Cover with plastic wrap, ensuring it touches the surface of the cream to prevent a skin from forming.

4. Fill the Choux:

- Once the choux pastries are completely cooled, use a pastry bag fitted with a small tip or a plain tip to fill each puff with the pastry cream.

5. Optional: Chocolate Ganache/Icing:

- If desired, you can dip the tops of the cream puffs in chocolate ganache or drizzle with chocolate icing.

6. Dust with Powdered Sugar:

- Dust the filled cream puffs with powdered sugar before serving.

7. Serve:

- Arrange the Choux à la Crème on a serving platter and enjoy these delightful pastries.

Tips:

- Ensure that the choux pastry is fully baked and has a hollow sound when tapped to ensure a light and airy texture.

- If making chocolate ganache, heat equal parts of heavy cream and chocolate until smooth for dipping or drizzling over the cream puffs.
- Experiment with different flavored pastry creams or add a touch of liqueur for a variation in flavor.

Sacristains

Ingredients:

      1 sheet of puff pastry (store-bought or homemade)
      1/2 cup granulated sugar
      1 teaspoon ground cinnamon
      1/4 cup unsalted butter, melted

Instructions:

1. Preheat Oven:

   - Preheat your oven to 375°F (190°C). Line a baking sheet with parchment paper.

2. Roll Out Puff Pastry:

   - If using store-bought puff pastry, roll out the sheet on a lightly floured surface to smooth out the seams.

3. Combine Sugar and Cinnamon:

   - In a small bowl, mix together the granulated sugar and ground cinnamon.

4. Brush with Melted Butter:

   - Brush the entire surface of the puff pastry sheet with melted butter.

5. Sprinkle with Sugar and Cinnamon:

   - Evenly sprinkle the sugar-cinnamon mixture over the buttered puff pastry.

6. Cut into Strips:

   - Using a sharp knife or a pizza cutter, cut the puff pastry into strips, about 1 inch wide.

7. Twist the Strips:

- Take each strip and twist it several times. This will create a spiral shape.

8. Arrange on Baking Sheet:

- Place the twisted strips on the prepared baking sheet, leaving space between each.

9. Bake:

- Bake in the preheated oven for approximately 12-15 minutes or until the sacristains are golden brown and puffed up.

10. Cool:

- Allow the sacristains to cool on the baking sheet for a few minutes.

11. Optional: Dust with Powdered Sugar:

- If desired, dust the sacristains with powdered sugar for a decorative touch.

12. Serve:

- Serve the sacristains warm or at room temperature.

13. Enjoy:

- Enjoy these delicious and flaky sacristains as a sweet treat with coffee or tea.

Tips:

- You can customize the flavor by adding a touch of orange zest or vanilla extract to the melted butter.
- Experiment with different sugar coatings, such as using brown sugar or a mixture of sugar and finely chopped nuts.

- These sacristains are best enjoyed on the day they are made for maximum freshness and crispiness.

Bouillabaisse Marseillaise (Fisherman's Stew)

Ingredients:

For the Broth:

    1 large onion, finely chopped
    1 leek, white part only, sliced
    2 fennel bulbs, sliced
    4 cloves garlic, minced
    2 tablespoons olive oil
    1 orange peel (wide strips, without pith)
    1 bouquet garni (thyme, bay leaves, parsley, tied together)
    1 teaspoon saffron threads
    1 teaspoon orange zest
    1 cup dry white wine
    1 can (28 oz) crushed tomatoes
    6 cups fish or seafood stock (or a combination of fish and vegetable stock)
    Salt and black pepper, to taste

For the Seafood:

14. 1 lb firm-fleshed white fish (such as cod or monkfish), cut into chunks

    1 lb shellfish (mussels, clams, or a combination), scrubbed and debearded
    1/2 lb small shrimp, peeled and deveined
    1/2 lb squid, cleaned and sliced into rings
    1/2 lb small octopus (optional), cleaned and cut into pieces

For the Rouille:

19. 2 large egg yolks

    2 cloves garlic, minced
    1 teaspoon Dijon mustard
    1/2 cup olive oil
    Salt and cayenne pepper, to taste

For Serving:

24. Slices of crusty bread (traditional rouille accompaniment)

   Fresh parsley, chopped (for garnish)

Instructions:

1. Prepare the Broth:

   - In a large pot, heat olive oil over medium heat. Add chopped onion, leek, fennel, and minced garlic. Sauté until softened.
   - Add orange peel, bouquet garni, saffron threads, and orange zest. Stir in white wine and allow it to reduce by half.
   - Add crushed tomatoes and fish or seafood stock. Season with salt and black pepper. Bring to a simmer and let it cook for about 20-30 minutes.

2. Prepare the Rouille:

   - In a bowl, whisk together egg yolks, minced garlic, and Dijon mustard.
   - Slowly drizzle in olive oil while whisking constantly to emulsify the mixture.
   - Season with salt and cayenne pepper to taste. Set aside.

3. Add Seafood to the Broth:

   - Once the broth has simmered and developed flavors, add the chunks of white fish, shellfish, shrimp, squid, and octopus (if using). Cook until the seafood is just cooked through and the shells of the shellfish have opened.

4. Serve:

   - Remove and discard the bouquet garni and orange peel. Ladle the bouillabaisse into serving bowls.

5. Toasted Bread:

- Serve the bouillabaisse with slices of crusty bread on the side.

6. Rouille:

- Spread rouille on the bread slices and float them on top of the bouillabaisse.

7. Garnish:

- Garnish with chopped fresh parsley.

8. Enjoy:

- Serve immediately and enjoy this rich and flavorful Bouillabaisse Marseillaise!

Tips:

- Choose a variety of fresh seafood based on availability and preference.
- Bouillabaisse is traditionally served with rouille-slathered bread, but you can also enjoy it with plain crusty bread.
- Adjust the spice level of the rouille by adding more or less cayenne pepper according to your preference.

Tarte aux Noix (Walnut Tart)

Ingredients:

For the Tart Crust:

    1 1/4 cups all-purpose flour
    1/2 cup unsalted butter, cold and diced
    1/4 cup granulated sugar
    1 large egg yolk
    1-2 tablespoons ice water

For the Walnut Filling:

6. 1 1/2 cups walnuts, finely chopped

    1/2 cup unsalted butter, melted
    1 cup granulated sugar
    3 large eggs
    1 teaspoon vanilla extract
    A pinch of salt

Instructions:

1. Prepare the Tart Crust:

- In a food processor, combine flour, cold diced butter, and sugar. Pulse until the mixture resembles coarse crumbs.
- Add the egg yolk and pulse again. Gradually add ice water, one tablespoon at a time, until the dough comes together.
- Form the dough into a disk, wrap it in plastic wrap, and refrigerate for at least 30 minutes.

2. Roll Out and Line Tart Pan:

- Preheat your oven to 375°F (190°C).

- On a floured surface, roll out the chilled dough into a circle large enough to fit a 9-inch tart pan. Transfer the rolled-out dough to the tart pan, pressing it gently into the bottom and up the sides. Trim any excess dough.

3. Pre-bake the Tart Crust:

    - Line the tart crust with parchment paper and fill it with pie weights or dried beans. Bake in the preheated oven for about 15 minutes.
    - Remove the parchment paper and weights and bake for an additional 5 minutes or until the crust is golden. Let it cool.

4. Prepare the Walnut Filling:

    - In a bowl, combine finely chopped walnuts, melted butter, sugar, eggs, vanilla extract, and a pinch of salt. Mix well until the filling is smooth and well combined.

5. Fill the Tart Shell:

    - Pour the walnut filling into the pre-baked tart shell, spreading it evenly.

6. Bake the Walnut Tart:

    - Bake in the preheated oven for 25-30 minutes or until the filling is set and the top is golden brown.

7. Cool and Serve:

    - Allow the Tarte aux Noix to cool in the tart pan on a wire rack. Once cooled, remove from the tart pan, slice, and serve.

8. Optional: Dust with Powdered Sugar:

    - Optionally, dust the top of the walnut tart with powdered sugar before serving for a decorative touch.

9. Enjoy:

- Enjoy the delicious and nutty flavor of Tarte aux Noix as a delightful dessert.

Tips:

- You can enhance the flavor by adding a splash of dark rum or brandy to the walnut filling.
- Serve the walnut tart with a dollop of whipped cream or a scoop of vanilla ice cream for a delightful treat.

Navettes de Marseille

Ingredients:

For the Dough:

    4 cups all-purpose flour
    1 cup granulated sugar
    1 cup unsalted butter, softened
    3 large eggs
    Zest of 1 orange
    1 teaspoon orange blossom water
    1 teaspoon active dry yeast (optional, for added leavening)
    A pinch of salt

For the Glaze:

9. 1 egg yolk

    1 tablespoon milk

Instructions:

1. Prepare the Dough:

- In a large mixing bowl, cream together the softened butter and sugar until light and fluffy.
- Add the eggs one at a time, beating well after each addition.
- Mix in the orange zest and orange blossom water.
- In a separate bowl, whisk together the flour and salt.
- Gradually add the dry ingredients to the wet ingredients, mixing until a soft dough forms.
- If using, dissolve the active dry yeast in a little warm water and add it to the dough. Knead until well combined.

2. Shape the Navettes:

- Preheat your oven to 350°F (175°C). Line baking sheets with parchment paper.
- Divide the dough into small portions and roll each portion into a thin log shape, about 4-5 inches long and 1/2 inch wide. Give each log a slight taper at the ends, resembling a boat shape (navette).

3. Egg Wash:

- In a small bowl, whisk together the egg yolk and milk to create an egg wash.

4. Glaze and Bake:

- Place the shaped navettes on the prepared baking sheets. Brush each navette with the egg wash for a golden finish.
- Bake in the preheated oven for 15-20 minutes or until the edges are lightly golden.

5. Cool:

- Allow the navettes to cool on a wire rack.

6. Optional: Orange Glaze (Traditional):

- For a traditional touch, you can prepare a simple orange glaze by combining powdered sugar with orange juice. Drizzle the glaze over the cooled navettes.

7. Serve:

- Once cooled and optionally glazed, serve the Navettes de Marseille.

8. Enjoy:

- Enjoy these delightful boat-shaped cookies with a hint of orange blossom water, a classic treat during the Candlemas season in Marseille.

Tips:

- The addition of active dry yeast is optional and can be omitted if you prefer a denser texture.
- Ensure the butter is softened but not melted for the right consistency of the dough.
- Experiment with different shapes or sizes for variation, but the classic boat shape is traditional for Navettes de Marseille.

Tarte Provençale

Ingredients:

For the Tart Dough:

    1 1/4 cups all-purpose flour
    1/2 cup unsalted butter, cold and diced
    1/4 cup grated Parmesan cheese
    1 large egg yolk
    2 tablespoons ice water
    A pinch of salt

For the Filling:

7. 2 tablespoons Dijon mustard

    1 large onion, thinly sliced
    2 medium-sized tomatoes, thinly sliced
    1 zucchini, thinly sliced
    1 eggplant, thinly sliced
    1 bell pepper (red or yellow), thinly sliced
    2 cloves garlic, minced
    1/4 cup olive oil
    Salt and black pepper, to taste
    Fresh herbs (thyme, rosemary, or basil) for garnish

Instructions:

1. Prepare the Tart Dough:

- In a food processor, combine flour, cold diced butter, grated Parmesan cheese, and a pinch of salt. Pulse until the mixture resembles coarse crumbs.
- Add the egg yolk and pulse again. Gradually add ice water, one tablespoon at a time, until the dough comes together.
- Form the dough into a disk, wrap it in plastic wrap, and refrigerate for at least 30 minutes.

2. Roll Out and Line Tart Pan:

- Preheat your oven to 375°F (190°C).
- On a floured surface, roll out the chilled dough into a circle large enough to fit a tart pan. Transfer the rolled-out dough to the tart pan, pressing it gently into the bottom and up the sides. Trim any excess dough.

3. Pre-bake the Tart Crust:

- Line the tart crust with parchment paper and fill it with pie weights or dried beans. Bake in the preheated oven for about 15 minutes.
- Remove the parchment paper and weights and bake for an additional 5 minutes or until the crust is golden. Let it cool.

4. Prepare the Filling:

- Spread Dijon mustard over the pre-baked tart crust.
- In a skillet, heat olive oil over medium heat. Add minced garlic and sliced onion. Sauté until the onion is softened.

5. Layer the Vegetables:

- Arrange the thinly sliced tomatoes, zucchini, eggplant, and bell pepper over the mustard-covered tart crust in an overlapping pattern.
- Drizzle olive oil over the layered vegetables. Season with salt and black pepper.

6. Bake:

- Bake the tart in the preheated oven for 30-40 minutes or until the vegetables are tender and the crust is golden brown.

7. Garnish:

- Garnish with fresh herbs like thyme, rosemary, or basil.

8. Serve:

- Allow the Tarte Provençale to cool slightly before slicing. Serve warm.

9. Enjoy:

- Enjoy this flavorful and colorful Provençal tart as a delightful appetizer or main dish.

Tips:

- Feel free to customize the vegetable selection based on seasonal availability.
- You can add a layer of grated cheese (such as Gruyère or mozzarella) over the mustard before arranging the vegetables for an extra layer of flavor.
- Experiment with different herbs and spices to suit your taste preferences.

Pain Complet (Whole Wheat Bread)

Ingredients:

For the Sponge:

    1 1/2 cups whole wheat flour
    1 cup warm water
    1 teaspoon active dry yeast

For the Bread Dough:

4. 2 1/2 cups whole wheat flour

    1 1/2 teaspoons salt
    1 tablespoon honey or maple syrup
    2 tablespoons olive oil or vegetable oil
    1 cup warm water (approximately)

Instructions:

1. Prepare the Sponge:

- In a mixing bowl, combine 1 1/2 cups of whole wheat flour, 1 cup of warm water, and active dry yeast. Mix well to form a thick batter.
- Cover the bowl with a clean kitchen towel and let the sponge rest in a warm place for about 30 minutes or until it becomes bubbly and active.

2. Mix the Dough:

- To the bubbly sponge, add the remaining whole wheat flour (2 1/2 cups), salt, honey or maple syrup, and olive oil.
- Gradually add warm water and knead the dough until it comes together. The amount of water may vary, so add it slowly until you achieve a smooth and slightly sticky dough.

3. Knead and Rise:

- Turn the dough out onto a floured surface and knead for about 8-10 minutes or until the dough is elastic and smooth.

- Place the dough in a lightly oiled bowl, cover with a kitchen towel, and let it rise in a warm place for 1-2 hours or until it doubles in size

4. Shape the Loaf:

    - Punch down the risen dough and shape it into a loaf. You can do this by rolling out the dough into a rectangle and then rolling it up tightly, sealing the seam.

5. Second Rise:

    - Place the shaped dough in a greased loaf pan. Cover it with a kitchen towel and let it rise for an additional 30-45 minutes.

6. Preheat the Oven:

    - Preheat your oven to 375°F (190°C) during the last 15 minutes of the second rise.

7. Bake:

    - Bake the whole wheat bread in the preheated oven for 25-30 minutes or until the top is golden brown and the loaf sounds hollow when tapped on the bottom.

8. Cool:

    - Allow the bread to cool in the pan for a few minutes before transferring it to a wire rack to cool completely.

9. Slice and Enjoy:

    - Once cooled, slice the Pain Complet and enjoy it with your favorite spreads or as a side to soups and salads.

Tips:

- Whole wheat flour tends to absorb more moisture than all-purpose flour, so adjust the water quantity accordingly.
- For added flavor, consider incorporating seeds or nuts into the dough, such as sunflower seeds or chopped walnuts.

- Store the bread in a sealed bag or container to keep it fresh. If the crust becomes too hard, you can refresh it by placing the bread in a 350°F (175°C) oven for a few minutes.

Pain Poilâne

Ingredients:

For the Leaven (Levain):

    1 cup whole wheat flour
    1/2 cup water
    1 tablespoon active sourdough starter

For the Dough:

4. 3 cups bread flour

    1 cup whole wheat flour
    1 1/2 cups water
    1 1/2 teaspoons salt

Instructions:

1. Prepare the Leaven (Levain):

- In a bowl, mix 1 cup of whole wheat flour with 1/2 cup of water and 1 tablespoon of active sourdough starter.
- Cover the bowl loosely and let it sit at room temperature for 8-12 hours or overnight until it becomes bubbly and active.

2. Mix the Dough:

- In a large mixing bowl, combine the bread flour, whole wheat flour, and salt.
- Add the leaven and water to the flour mixture. Mix until you have a shaggy dough.

3. Autolyse:

- Let the dough rest for 30 minutes to 1 hour. This allows the flour to fully hydrate and the gluten to start developing.

4. Knead the Dough:

- Knead the dough for about 10-15 minutes until it becomes smooth and elastic. You can do this by hand or using a stand mixer with a dough hook attachment.

5. Bulk Fermentation:

- Place the kneaded dough in a lightly oiled bowl, cover it, and let it rise at room temperature for 3-4 hours. During this time, perform a series of stretch and folds every 30 minutes for the first 2 hours.

6. Shape the Dough:

- After the bulk fermentation, turn the dough out onto a floured surface and shape it into a round boule.

7. Final Proof:

- Place the shaped dough in a floured proofing basket (banneton) or a bowl lined with a floured cloth. Cover and let it proof for 2-3 hours or until it has visibly expanded.

8. Preheat the Oven:

- Preheat your oven to 475°F (245°C) with a Dutch oven or a baking stone inside.

9. Score the Dough:

- Once the oven is preheated, carefully transfer the dough to the hot Dutch oven or baking stone. Score the top of the dough with a sharp knife.

10. Bake:

- Cover the Dutch oven with a lid and bake for 20 minutes. Remove the lid and continue baking for an additional 20-25 minutes or until the bread has a deep golden brown crust.

11. Cool:

- Allow the Pain Poilâne to cool on a wire rack before slicing.

12. Enjoy:

- Slice and enjoy the delicious, rustic flavor of your homemade Pain Poilâne.

Tips:

- Adjust the water quantity as needed, depending on the hydration level of your sourdough starter and the absorption of your flours.
- Experiment with different ratios of whole wheat and bread flour to achieve the desired texture and flavor.
- For added flavor, you can incorporate seeds or nuts into the dough during the mixing stage.

Pain de Campagne

Ingredients:

For the Leaven (Levain):

    1 cup bread flour
    1/2 cup whole wheat flour
    1/2 cup water
    2 tablespoons active sourdough starter

For the Dough:

5. 3 cups bread flour

    1 cup whole wheat flour
    1 1/2 cups water
    1 1/2 teaspoons salt

Instructions:

1. Prepare the Leaven (Levain):

- In a bowl, mix 1 cup of bread flour, 1/2 cup of whole wheat flour, 1/2 cup of water, and 2 tablespoons of active sourdough starter.
- Cover the bowl loosely and let it sit at room temperature for 8-12 hours or overnight until it becomes bubbly and active.

2. Mix the Dough:

- In a large mixing bowl, combine 3 cups of bread flour, 1 cup of whole wheat flour, and salt.
- Add the leaven and water to the flour mixture. Mix until you have a shaggy dough.

3. Autolyse:

- Let the dough rest for 30 minutes to 1 hour. This allows the flour to fully hydrate and the gluten to start developing.

4. Knead the Dough:

    - Knead the dough for about 10-15 minutes until it becomes smooth and elastic. You can do this by hand or using a stand mixer with a dough hook attachment.

5. Bulk Fermentation:

    - Place the kneaded dough in a lightly oiled bowl, cover it, and let it rise at room temperature for 3-4 hours. During this time, perform a series of stretch and folds every 30 minutes for the first 2 hours.

6. Shape the Dough:

    - After the bulk fermentation, turn the dough out onto a floured surface and shape it into a round boule.

7. Final Proof:

    - Place the shaped dough in a floured proofing basket (banneton) or a bowl lined with a floured cloth. Cover and let it proof for 2-3 hours or until it has visibly expanded.

8. Preheat the Oven:

    - Preheat your oven to 475°F (245°C) with a Dutch oven or a baking stone inside.

9. Score the Dough:

    - Once the oven is preheated, carefully transfer the dough to the hot Dutch oven or baking stone. Score the top of the dough with a sharp knife.

10. Bake:

- Cover the Dutch oven with a lid and bake for 20 minutes. Remove the lid and continue baking for an additional 20-25 minutes or until the bread has a deep golden brown crust.

11. Cool:

    - Allow the Pain de Campagne to cool on a wire rack before slicing.

12. Enjoy:

    - Slice and enjoy the rustic and flavorful Pain de Campagne.

Tips:

- Adjust the water quantity as needed, depending on the hydration level of your sourdough starter and the absorption of your flours.
- For added flavor, you can incorporate seeds or grains into the dough during the mixing stage.
- Experiment with different ratios of whole wheat and bread flour to achieve the desired texture and flavor.

Bugnes

Ingredients:

For the Dough:

>   4 cups all-purpose flour
>   1/2 cup unsalted butter, softened
>   1/2 cup granulated sugar
>   4 large eggs
>   1/4 teaspoon salt
>   Zest of 1 lemon
>   1/4 cup milk
>   1 teaspoon vanilla extract
>   Vegetable oil for frying

For Dusting:

10. Powdered sugar

Instructions:

1. Prepare the Dough:

   - In a large mixing bowl, combine the softened butter and granulated sugar. Cream them together until light and fluffy.
   - Add the eggs one at a time, beating well after each addition.
   - Mix in the salt and lemon zest.
   - Gradually add the flour, alternating with the milk, and continue mixing.
   - Add the vanilla extract and knead the dough until it comes together. It should be soft and elastic.

2. Rest the Dough:

   - Cover the dough with plastic wrap and let it rest in the refrigerator for at least 1 hour.

3. Roll and Cut:

   - On a floured surface, roll out the chilled dough to a thickness of about 1/4 inch.

- Cut the dough into strips or diamond shapes using a knife or a fluted pastry cutter.

4. Heat the Oil:

- In a deep fryer or a heavy-bottomed pot, heat vegetable oil to 350°F (175°C).

5. Fry the Bugnes:

- Carefully fry the bugnes in batches until they are golden brown on both sides. This usually takes about 2-3 minutes per side.
- Use a slotted spoon to remove them from the oil and place them on a paper towel-lined plate to absorb any excess oil.

6. Dust with Powdered Sugar:

- While the bugnes are still warm, generously dust them with powdered sugar. You can do this by placing the sugar in a fine-mesh sieve and sifting it over the bugnes.

7. Serve:

- Bugnes are best enjoyed fresh and warm. Serve them as a delightful treat with a cup of coffee or tea.

8. Enjoy:

- Enjoy these light and sweet Bugnes, a traditional French pastry especially popular during Carnival season.

Tips:

- Be cautious when frying to avoid overcrowding the pan and ensure even cooking.
- Customize the flavor by adding a hint of nutmeg or orange zest to the dough.
- Experiment with different shapes and sizes for a playful presentation.

Pain de Mie (White Sandwich Bread)

Ingredients:

For the Bread Dough:

    4 cups bread flour
    2 teaspoons active dry yeast
    1 1/2 teaspoons salt
    2 tablespoons sugar
    1 1/4 cups warm milk
    1/4 cup unsalted butter, softened

For the Egg Wash (optional):

7. 1 egg, beaten

    1 tablespoon water

Instructions:

1. Activate the Yeast:

- In a small bowl, combine the warm milk, sugar, and active dry yeast. Let it sit for about 5-10 minutes or until the mixture becomes frothy.

2. Mix the Dough:

- In a large mixing bowl, combine the bread flour and salt. Create a well in the center and pour in the activated yeast mixture.
- Add the softened butter and knead the dough until it comes together. You can use a stand mixer with a dough hook attachment or knead by hand on a floured surface.

3. Knead and Rise:

- Knead the dough for about 10-15 minutes until it becomes smooth and elastic. Place the dough in a lightly oiled bowl, cover it with a kitchen towel, and let it rise in a warm place for 1-2 hours or until it doubles in size.

4. **Shape the Loaf:**

   - Punch down the risen dough and turn it out onto a floured surface. Flatten the dough into a rectangle and then roll it up tightly, sealing the seam.

5. **Place in Loaf Pan:**

   - Grease a standard-sized loaf pan and place the shaped dough into the pan, seam side down.

6. **Second Rise:**

   - Cover the loaf pan with a kitchen towel and let the dough rise for an additional 30-45 minutes or until it reaches the top of the pan.

7. **Preheat the Oven:**

   - Preheat your oven to 375°F (190°C) during the last 15 minutes of the second rise.

8. **Egg Wash (optional):**

   - In a small bowl, beat the egg with water. Brush the top of the risen dough with the egg wash for a shiny finish (this step is optional).

9. **Bake:**

   - Place the loaf pan in the preheated oven and bake for 25-30 minutes or until the top is golden brown and the bread sounds hollow when tapped on the bottom.

10. **Cool:**

    - Allow the Pain de Mie to cool in the pan for a few minutes, then transfer it to a wire rack to cool completely.

11. **Slice and Enjoy:**

    - Once cooled, slice the Pain de Mie into even slices and enjoy it for sandwiches or toast.

Tips:

- Adjust the sweetness by increasing or decreasing the sugar according to your preference.
- For a softer crust, you can cover the bread with a clean kitchen towel while it cools.
- Store the bread in a sealed bag or container to keep it fresh.